MUSIC
AND ITS
STORY

MUSIC
AND ITS STORY

PERCY M. YOUNG

Drawings by Reginald Haggar

LUTTERWORTH PRESS
LONDON

First published 1960

COPYRIGHT © 1960 PERCY M. YOUNG

PRINTED IN GREAT BRITAIN
BY WESTERN PRINTING SERVICES LTD., BRISTOL

Contents

Introduction

IT HAS always seemed to me during a long experience of teaching, and talking about, music that the general music-lover, whether young or old, is not at ease with the history of music. The reason, I suspect, is that the History of Music tends to become a thing apart, worse still a "subject". It is, in truth, history; a record of human behaviour and ideas under certain conditions—which themselves are always changing. The music practised at any time takes the pattern it assumes because social and economic developments thus decreed it. In learning of these relationships we learn more about people (which is the reason for history being written and studied in the first place), more about music, and more *of* music. In respect of the music itself we can imaginatively put ourselves within the experience of those for whom particular works were first intended, and so approach it with fresh minds and without the prejudices of our own time and environment.

The main prejudices are of this order. We listen to "old" music with tolerance, not expecting it to be as clever or as exhilarating as "modern" music. Or, conversely, we reject new music because it is not so "attractive" as that of former times. If, however, we can see why music was appreciated, or understood, by particular communities (whether we "like" it or not) we add an extra dimension to our own understanding.

Compared with architecture, literature, or painting, music appears to be a young art. So we were once told in rather firm tones. Music, however, so far from being the

7

youngest is probably the oldest of the arts. This being so we should extend our interest as far back as possible, for it is from the oldest music of the earliest civilizations that the power of expression developed; while some attitudes of our own day cannot be understood unless placed in the human context. We may decide, in fact, that music, depending on emotions which change little, defies history.

That brings us to this point: that music is a part of history (although unwarrantably neglected by historians), but it is—music. We do not learn music from reading books, but from listening to or taking part in it. It is to be hoped, therefore, that those who use this book will not neglect to set actual first-hand experience into the text at the right points. In the Appendix is a selected list of recordings; but I like to think that as far as possible my readers will take an active part in playing or singing such of the works mentioned in the course of the story as are practicable (and that is a great many). This, I believe, is the only sure way to feel what musical values really are.

Within the space at my disposal I have not found room to discuss in any detail what is called Musical Form. Here again are misconceptions. Musical Form (usually set out in capital letters) stimulates a certain mechanical or mathematical aptitude, but not necessarily an affection for music. Indeed a too-conscious concentration on form, which produces a way of looking at or listening to parts rather than wholes, can hinder our understanding. Anyway, composers—even though they have an eye on what their friends are doing—make their own forms, and no two works are identical in structure. This brings us back to where we started. A work of art is unique, created out of an imagination and intelligence which is brought to that point of creation by forces outside of itself—by history.

History, as has been suggested, is a whole and not the

sum of separate parts. We may not at any one time find it easy to look on it so—simply because opportunity is not limitless; but we can try. The history with which this book deals is also written in other ways—in buildings, in paintings, in sculptures, in ceramics—and Mr. Haggar's illustrations are intended to send you further afield in exploring the visual arts.

This is another means whereby the past can be turned into the present, and by which history can be experienced as a living, as well as a lively, interest. The moral of this book (if there is one) is that you are the maker of history as well as the next person: what to me is more important is that you are the one who must keep music as a living art.

In one of his essays Francis Bacon wrote: "In the youth of a state arms do flourish; in the middle age of a state, learning; and then both of them together for a time; in the declining age of a state, mechanical arts and merchandise."

This (which also has a moral) runs alongside my story: by interpreting "mechanical arts" rather differently from the seventeenth-century author we see some hint of why modern civilizations may decline.

Art means doing. This book is written for artists, not Artists.

P.M.Y.

March 1960

1

Music in Ancient Times

PEOPLE sing and dance; they often accompany their
singing and dancing with sounds obtained from whatever sound-making objects—maybe of wood, of bone, or
of shell—are to hand. The instruments thus used may also
fulfil a separate function—to encourage, to frighten, or
merely to entertain. In the relation of such activities to
human society lies the story of music.

In the ordinary way the telling of this story tends to be
unconvincing, for it frequently seems that whereas music
was once very simple it has gradually become more and
more complex—and therefore "better". At the present
time, however, there are sufficient critics of "modern
music" amongst us to make us question this idea. Modern
music—that is any music written by a living composer—is
unwelcome to many of our friends. They say, in general
terms, that such music is "ugly", that it doesn't make
sense, that they can't understand it.

On the other hand the very same people complain of
music that comes from a rather distant past—say from the
Middle Ages—in almost exactly the same language. The
truth is that, unconsciously, they are more than a little
afraid. Music exerts a profound influence on behaviour; it
affects the emotions as powerfully as do drugs. As the
causes of such effects are unknown—even to scientific in-
vestigators—the musician is still regarded by many as first

cousin to a magician. "There is", says the enthusiast applauding a good pianist, "magic in his fingers." There is, of course, nothing of the sort, but that there might appear to be is a sufficient reason for a common way of thinking.

In olden times there were no two ways about it. The musician *was* a magician, and he was often regarded with the same degree of awe and rewarded with the same tokens of respect and fear. We flatter ourselves that we have outgrown the primitive state. But we haven't entirely.

Contemporary popular music is sometimes violently stimulating through noisy emphasis on simple, repetitive rhythmic patterns, or exploitation of curious, inescapable colour-effects. Or it drools monotonously and without apparent meaning until we are, as it were, anæsthetized. In a different way much modern "highbrow" music can arrive at the same end. Thus both are held under suspicion, though not always by the same persons.

The contemporary composer, like the contemporary painter and sculptor, has become aware of primitive activity, and on the whole his art has benefited. One does not base one's æsthetic enjoyment only on reason. An artist is not wholly reasonable as he creates. The value of studying primitive art is that it enables us to see part of the reason for unreason. It explains something of our own nature. It shows the source of all human endeavour in the field of what is called art. And it can help to keep our appreciation as well as our own self-expression somewhere near to its roots.

At the same time this does not give us the licence to defy the whole of our heritage and culture, and to ape the primitive. When we do this consciously—either for personal gain or easy notoriety—we are behaving against our nature and our environment; and that is what no primitive artist (so far as we know) ever did. The beauty of true folk-music (unhelped by well-meaning editors), as of the native sculpture of the African Ivory Coast, or the prehistoric cave-pictures at Altamira in Spain, is in its integrity.

The beginning of music is remote. It always was remote. In earlier times the patient, scholarly search for origin was unknown. Speculation and historical research were represented by a free-flying fancy and imagination. The general tendency of ancient races was to load the responsibility for inventing music on to the gods, and it must be confessed that the legends enshrining such ideas were singularly attractive.

A Mexican tribe preserved through the ages one such myth, in which music was drawn from the sun by the god Tezcatlipoca. To enable it to reach the earth he built a bridge of whales and turtles across the sky, on which were carried drums and other instruments. An Indian story names the first musician as the tribal god Lingo, who not only possessed all the eighteen instruments (string, woodwind, brass, and percussion) known to the tribe, but also played them all at once.

To the Hebrews of Old Testament times the founder of music was Jubal. To the Greeks of the classical period Apollo and Orpheus were the great supernatural musicians.

It is not surprising then that music was from the earliest times used as a medium whereby the gods might be placated, or praised.

Practice, however, comes before theory; and music existed long before theories regarding its existence. The first form of music to take shape was vocal, for song grew naturally from speech. Indeed it may be argued that

13

Engraved armour, 650 B.C.

speech is a form of music, in that the emotional content of a message is contained less in a sequence of words than in the rhythm and the inflection—the rise and fall—which the speaker gives to his word patterns. In a sense the beginnings of music are always with us. On the one hand small children invent their own melodic idioms; on the other, native tribes, living far from the centres of Western culture, preserve the habits of thousands of years ago.

The Bantu tribes who live south of the equator in Africa, for instance, have a living tradition of folk-music taking us back to long before the establishment of the music that is familiar to us. Their songs closely follow the rhythms of speech. Their melodies are kept within a small range, often of no more than five sounds. Such limitation is practicable, for a confined melody, to which the attached words are considered significant, is more readily memorized. The same consideration applies to much popular music of our own tradition, and the great composers often achieve general immortality through an impressive economy in melodic outline.

Primitive vocal music of whatever origin is basically simple. But it is inevitable that man experiments, so solo singing, or unison singing, may easily expand into the obvious form of part-singing, in which a second voice, or a second group of voices, sings the given melody at a higher or lower pitch. This form of parallel singing was a feature of medieval music in Europe, but it was to be found in much earlier times, just as it is now to be heard under tribal conditions.

It is also common to hear tribal music with accompaniment; this being supplied by drums or rattles, by kinds of lutes, lyres, harps, xylophones, flutes, panpipes. . . . There is an infinite number of possibilities here, according to the inventiveness of the people concerned and the material available. For obvious reasons the earliest types of accompaniment are primarily percussive, but none the less effective and colourful. At the present time there is a fascinating field for exploration in this respect in New Guinea, where Australian scholars are doing valuable work.

Song may be regarded as the first-comer into the field of music. Percussion instruments, however, have an early place. Through song man may communicate; so too through the orderly arrangement of rhythmic patterns. The sound of a drum will carry for long distances, and drum patterns were, and are, used significantly: a simple code may spell the onset of danger, another its termination. In present military ritual the drums have a place of honour, less because of their musical character than of their importance in communication.

The sounds of music (until the recent development of recording instruments) were perishable, but, in a limited way, other aspects of the art were not.

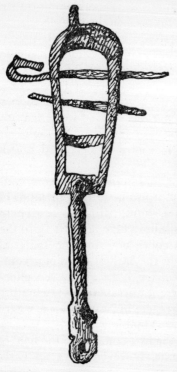

Sistrum (rings missing), c. 1600 B.C.

The discoveries of archæologists tell us something of the music of former times. In his excavations in Egypt, Sir Flinders Petrie unearthed clappers: one pair made of wood, another of bone. These belonged to the second millennium before Christ. From the same country and the same period have come other percussion instruments, including the *sistrum* (a number of rings or cups threaded on rods on which they will jangle when shaken) which was used particularly in the cult of the goddess Isis. Bone flutes of the neolithic age have been preserved in the peat deposits of Denmark, and there are examples of Irish bronze-age trumpets.

Pictures are another source of information. Bushmen drawings in South Africa show the musical use of shooting bows. Cave drawings and rock carvings in different parts of India show many instruments which are still in use there. There are stringed instruments—harps played with bows, zithers, lutes; woodwind (or nearly related) instruments—flutes and conch-shells; brass—in the form of trumpets; and percussion—a large variety, including clappers, castanets, bells, gongs, rattles, drums. The orchestra as a more or less disciplined body of instrumentalists has a recorded history of, perhaps, four thousand years, in which Western music occupies in point of time only a small part. It is, however, only in post-Renaissance Western music that the orchestra has come to have a separate and individual function. In earlier music, as in native and Oriental music of our time, instruments were employed either to support voices or to fulfil some other apparently practical purpose.

The organization of musical sounds into recognizable units of meaning was through song, and therefore through melody. At this point attention should be drawn to the two poles of melody. The power to invent melody is universal. There is nothing to prevent anyone making up a melody, which may consist of sounds of any pitch and in any, or no, particular rhythm. A private impulse to melody may produce strange results, which have no connection with rules or systems. Broadly speaking, this is the source of "rhapsodic" melody, of the side of music now described as Romantic. On the other hand, a melody which is designed for a ritual, and therefore for repetition, or for singing by many people, must be relatively simple and orderly. It must be governed by acceptable principles. This, then, leads us to the root of classical order and restraint.

Each community develops its own tradition of folk-music, which may or may not (according to geographical considerations) overlap that of other communities. At the present time, however, it is only in places to which industry and technology has not fully extended that an unbroken tradition may be examined. Thus we may profitably move from the urbanized west to the east of Europe; to Armenia, where the folk-musical tradition is one of the most ancient and one of the richest to be found. What is still commonplace in Armenia shows a pattern that was once universal.

Stone slab of a kist at Kivik, Sweden, Bronze age

Peasant music in Armenia accompanied work in the fields and in the house. There were songs of the plough, shepherd songs and pipe music, songs relating to spinning and cooking, and cradle songs. There were songs for the seasons of the year, songs to celebrate or commemorate birth, marriage, and death. In such songs the melodic phrases, closely linked to verbal rhythms, were short and often repeated, tending to centre on one sound, which was therefore made to appear more important than the others. But singers would vary the familiar patterns by extemporized ornaments. These extemporizations might include references to the passing scene either through the inclusion of additional and apt words or through more or less descriptive noises. The singer might (to the possible delight of his friends) make what we might now call a cadenza to imitate a cow, or a bird, or the noise of a wagon.

The professional singer in Armenia has at all times sung of the legends and heroes of ancient times, and his inventiveness has always been a source of wonderment and delight. To this day such singers, akin to the minstrels and bards of old, sing famous stories—as of David of Sasun, who lived a thousand years ago—to the workers on collective farms.

The songs of Armenia are often accompanied by instruments peculiar to that country, such as the *saz*, a form of small guitar; the *tarr*, somewhat like a lute; the *kya mancha*, similar to a banjo but played with a bow; and the *darr*, a tambourine.

Such music is studied and preserved, and singers are encouraged to continue in the same tradition, by the Soviet Government; and Russian composers often make use of the melodies and rhythmic idioms to be found in it.

So far as we in the West are concerned such music lies in the outskirts of our experience, but from time to time we shall return to it, for it has always existed to exert more or less of an influence on "art music".

Certain traditions have proved more important than

others, for the musical organization of great civilizations has led to practices and theories which have become part of the texture of all our musical appreciation and understanding.

In Egypt in ancient times music was highly regarded, for it was thought that the sound made by any object was its voice—its spirit. By the use of such "voices", it was argued, the unseen forces of nature might be influenced. Four thousand years ago music in that country was widely cultivated, and ritual chants were regularly sung in the

From an Egyptian wall-painting, c. 2000 B.C.

temples, accompanied by such instruments as *sistra*, flutes, and reed-pipes. In the second millennium before Christ there were not only professional male but also female musicians, who were employed for both secular and religious occasions. Egyptian music absorbed other influences through war, immigration, and trading connections, and among these were the musical idioms of Syria, Persia, Babylon, and Assyria.

The Old Testament tells us much about the place of music in Hebrew life across the long period of time from about 3000 B.C. to two hundred or so years before Christ.

In the Book of Exodus it is recorded how Moses came down from the Mount of Sinai with the tablets of stone on which were the Commandments, and how the people were singing and dancing. The songs and dances were extremely noisy (for Joshua had thought the sounds to be of a battle), and Moses was very angry. In the Book of Numbers we are given a glimpse of a work song, sung while the people were digging for water. In the first verse of Isaiah 5 is a reference to a narrative song, the song of a vineyard. Another narrative song is that ascribed to Deborah in the Book of Judges. Among the famous musical characters of the Old Testament were Jubal, "the father of all such as handle the harp and the pipe" (Genesis 4: 21); Miriam, the sister of Moses, who "took a timbrel in her hand; and all the women went out after her with timbrels and with dances" (Exodus 15: 20); Jephthah's daughter was also a timbrel player and dancer (Judges 11: 34); while Nebuchadnezzar employed a complete company of musicians—playing "cornet, flute, harp, sackbut, psaltery, and dulcimer, and all kinds of music"—to induce the proper worship of his golden image (Daniel 3: 4). The most important musician, however, was David, who not only played the harp to cure

King Saul of his madness, but was popularly supposed to have composed the Psalms.

The Psalms were, in fact, the work of many poets and musicians, and their composition was spread over many centuries. This is the case with any liturgical music—the Psalms were the principal part of the worship of the Temple in Jerusalem—as reference to the index of any hymnal will show. Until the destruction of the Second Temple in the year A.D. 70 Jewish music was in the hands of trained musicians and was very varied. Trumpets and cymbals marked the climaxes of ceremonial sacrifice; solemn passages of Scripture were chanted according to ancient tradition from which no deviation was permitted; and the Psalms were sung to melodies arranged within clearly defined groups.

The Psalms vary in poetic form. Some are designed for solo voices; some for solo answered by chorus; some are fully choral; some have the form of a litany. From the poetic structures grew musical forms, and melodies were also organized according to what we might now call mode or key. At the head of the Psalms, as shown in the Old Testament, are frequently set instructions which may relate either to the vocal melody or to the instrumental accompaniment. Instrumental accompaniments—as in ritual music in ancient India and China—were invariably embellishments of the melodies, and not arranged "in parts", or "in harmony", as in modern times.

Although the classic Jewish tradition of music was broken at the time of the destruction of the Second Temple the manner in which the Psalms were sung would appear to have lingered on, and in some way or other to have influenced the development of the earliest forms of chant in the Christian Church. In any case, because the Psalms became the central part of Christian worship their distinctive poetic forms dictated the basic structure of the first liturgical music of the West.

This was not all. The Jews attributed certain qualities to music itself, believing that from "strong" music came strength, and from "weak" music weakness. Music, in fact, was thought to exercise moral power, and this idea, in one form or another, is still with us. Thus "decadent" music (what is "decadent" is normally decided by a committee acting on behalf of the Government) is banned in the Soviet system; and certain types of music (usually stated to be "too secular") are either forbidden or discouraged by various churches elsewhere.

Many theories concerning music come from the Greeks, who, in classical times, gave serious consideration to the art in all its aspects. Homer, the reputed author of the

Greek street musicians, from a mosaic at Pompeii

Iliad and the *Odyssey*, was said to have been a singer, a minstrel; and from the tenth century before Christ, when he is thought to have lived, down to the Christian era poetry and music were indissolubly linked together. As in Jewish music poetic rhythms dictated those of melody. Thus Greek music differed from most of the music with which we are familiar because its rhythms were based on quantity rather than on stress—a similar contrast exists between Latin and English poetry. Melodies, used in drama and religious festivals, were also organized into scales or modes. Of instruments, the Greeks had a relatively restricted range and they are familiar through frequent representation on vases and sculptures.

The main division was between lyres and pipes—strings and woodwind. In Homeric times the lyres possessed only three or four strings. By the fifth century B.C., however, they had five or seven. Legend says that the inventor of the seven-string lyre was Terpander, the musician-politician who, in the seventh century, was summoned by the Delphic oracle to Sparta to pacify the disordered state. Because he was a musician he was considered eminently the proper person to undertake such a task.

The lyre was principally the instrument of the amateurs. Professional players used the *kithara*. For the most part these string instruments were employed to accompany song.

The pipes—called *auloi*—were normally reed instruments of the oboe family, and frequently they were played in pairs. One gave a melody, the other a drone note—as on the bagpipes. Percussion was limited to dances of Oriental nature, such as those which celebrated the feast day of the god of wine, Dionysus.

The Greeks, from whom we derive many of the notable features of our civilization, were great searchers after truth; they were also great law-givers and anxious to

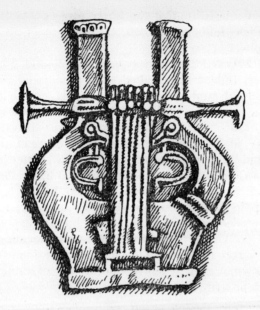

Lyre, from a Greek tetradrachm, 360 B.C.

impose order on a chaotic world. In respect of music they fully explored its scientific properties, so that the mathematician Pythagoras was considered one of the first authorities on acoustics. It was he who discovered the mathematical relationship between the principal consonant intervals of octave, fifth, and fourth. In the fifth century there was in Athens a school of musical theorists who codified scales and rhythms. One result of all this work was a general expansion of musical technique, rather as in the time of Bach the new system of "equal temperament" in tuning keyboard instruments affected the form and character of music; another was the further consideration of the place music should occupy in education. One

25

who particularly studied the latter project was Damon, whose ideas influenced Plato, the greatest of all Greek philosophers.

Plato believed that music had a profound effect on character. Indeed he specified what modes and rhythms were helpful and harmful respectively to character-building. He indicated that while musicians were persons of importance they should be subject to direction by authority; and he laid great stress on the place of music in education. "Can we", he wrote, "find any better [education] than the old-fashioned sort, gymnastic for the body and music for the soul?" Music to Plato, however, was of wider application than it is with us, for it involved all the higher intellectual training, including literature.

Echoes of Greek thought of music and education have carried across the ages. A quotation from John Milton shows how powerful he felt the moral force of music to be. We hear, he writes,

> . . . sometimes the lute or soft organ stop waiting on elegant voices, either to religious, martial, or civil ditties; which if wise men and prophets be not extremely out, have a great power over dispositions and manners, to smooth and make them gentle from rustic harshness and distempered passions.

That is derived from Greek teaching. So also is this, from Thomas Carlyle:

> The Greeks fabled of Sphere-Harmonies [the music of the spheres was a tempting subject for speculation by Greek musicians, mathematicians and astronomers]; it was the feeling they had of the inner structure of Nature; that the soul of all her voices and utterances was perfect music. Poetry, therefore, we will call *Musical Thought*. The Poet is he who *thinks* in that manner. At bottom, it bears still on power and intellect; it is a man's sincerity and depth of vision that makes him a Poet. See deep enough, and you see

musically; the heart of Nature *being* everywhere music, if you can only reach it.

The fact that music has a place in modern education is another reflection of the Greek outlook; it is there not because it is, or might be, entertaining, but because it is thought to be "valuable". Whether it is or not depends on

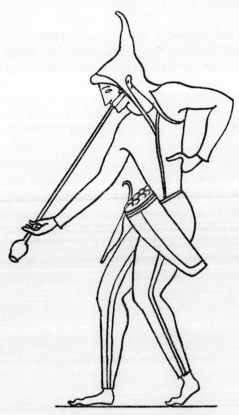

Greek trumpeter, from an earthenware plate,
c. 520 B.C.

numerous factors: so too, presumably, in the Athenian system of more than two thousand years ago.

What was Greek music like? Mostly we can only guess at such reconstructions of style and performance as are given by writers. But a few actual pieces remain; for the Greeks (like the Indians, the Egyptians, and the Chinese) used a system of alphabetical letters as a form of musical notation.

There are fragments of dramatic melody on papyri of the fourth and the third centuries B.C. There are two Hymns to Apollo inscribed on stone during the second century, and discovered by French archæologists in 1893. There is a drinking song discovered at Tralles in Asia Minor. There are pagan hymns belonging to the first century of the Christian era which survived in manuscripts of theoretical works. In all, however, there are not more than a dozen examples, and of these only one is instrumental.

The tradition of Greek practical music virtually disappeared. What happened to it will be considered in the next chapter. But the Greek love of music is reflected in a number of words which we apply to music, without which we should be in difficulties; for they are Greek words. The most familiar are—melody, harmony, and rhythm; as well as symphony and orchestra. These words, perhaps, help to make what is remote rather less remote.

2

The Beginning of the Western Tradition

IN the fourth century before Christ Greek customs and culture were carried far from the land of their origin through the military achievements of Philip of Macedon and his son Alexander the Great. Greek was spoken in India on the one hand and in Egypt, where the great city of Alexandria was established, on the other. Greek music accompanied the other arts to these distant outposts, there to mingle with what was already in existence. Herodotus and Plato had in their day admired Egyptian music, but by the first century B.C. the Sicilian-Greek historian Diodorus positively informs us that the Greeks were borrowing from Egyptian musical techniques. This was particularly the case in respect of the ritual music for the worship of the goddess Isis, whose cult by some Greeks led to the erection of temples in her honour in Greece. In this form of worship, as in all others, it was essential that the music should be authentic.

The power of the Greeks faded and their domination of the Mediterranean and Ægean world was replaced by that of the ambitious Romans, to whom the Greeks became subject. The Romans rapidly extended their Empire. The Danube became one frontier, the Rhine another, and in the first century of the Christian era Britain was colonized; so that all of what we now term Western Europe, together with the Balkan countries, Palestine, Syria, Asia Minor, and the north coast of Africa, were bound together in a confederation of which the centre was Rome. The Romans built cities, both splendid and comfortable, roads over which armies and merchants might swiftly and purposefully move; they established order and imposed a system of government and of law. The common use of the Latin tongue made intercourse between different peoples and cultures possible and profitable, and was an important—perhaps the most important—factor in the ultimate development of European music.

In comparison with the Greeks, however, the Romans were not, as we would say, very musical. They were content in the first place to import their music from Greece, as the British in the nineteenth century willingly accepted vast supplies of German music. The wind instruments, the lyres and citharas (the latter being one of the instruments which the Emperor Nero is likely to have played), familiar in Greece became commonplace in public and private entertainments in Rome. Musical competitions after Greek models were instituted by Nero. Brass instruments on the other hand were independently developed for military service, and examples of *tuba*, *lituus*, and *buccina* (which were also represented on sculptures) are still in existence. One other instrument, of greater interest, was in high favour: the organ.

Here again is a Greek word, and we know that an instrument based on the same principles as the modern (non-electronic!) organ was in use in northern Africa at least two or three centuries before Christ. In 1885 a model of an early organ was excavated on the site of the ancient city of Carthage. In 1931 the remains of a Roman organ were found near Budapest, and an inscription stated that it had been played by a Roman legionary and also his wife. The organ of this period was also known as the *hydraulus*,

Buccina and tuba, Trajan's Column, Rome

because the supply of wind to the pipes was regulated by
water pressure. The *hydraulus* was in constant use until
about the fifth or sixth century, but it was then entirely a
secular instrument, played in amphitheatres and other
places of entertainment as well as for private pleasure. It
was disliked, on account of its more ribald associations,
equally by Jews and Christians, and with the rise of
Christianity it fell into disuse, until its revival in the ninth
century.

In the third century Rome ceased to be the capital of
the Roman Empire. The greatest of the emperors of that
age was Diocletian, who held his court at Nicomedeia in

Asia Minor. By this time there was a substantial minority of Christian believers, accustomed to regular communal worship, among the citizens of the Empire. It has been said that the Christians made one-fifth of the whole. Christianity of those days was marked by the absorption of many ideas and practices that were not unfamiliar to followers of other cults, particularly of Judaism, Mithraism, and Stoicism.

Music had from apostolic times played a vigorous part in promoting and preserving the new faith, and it too had many roots. It is clear that in the early organization of Christian music much was adapted from the tradition of the synagogue. Thus the Psalms were taken over, together with the general method of singing them to simple chants arranged in various modes. From the synagogue also came the hymn *Sanctus, sanctus, sanctus* ("Holy, holy, holy"), and *Gratias agimus tibi, Domine* ("We give thanks to thee, O Lord"), which later became part of the order of the Mass. In addition to these traditional forms of worship new works were created, particularly hymns (also a Greek word) of a more lyrical character. Of these the prototypes were the canticles, *Benedictus, Magnificat*, and *Nunc Dimittis*, as recorded in the Gospel of St. Luke. The existence of a wide collection of sacred music is testified by various references to "psalms, hymns, and spiritual songs" in the Epistles of St. Paul.

In the first three or four centuries of Christianity there was a general measure of freedom in regard to music, and the style of hymn singing in particular was strongly influenced by local traditions and practices. There is one tangible piece of evidence denoting Greek influence, for one fragment of Greek notation preserved in an Egyptian papyrus of the third century is a Christian hymn.

In the fourth century the adoption of Christianity as the

official religion of the Empire, and the regulation of its doctrine by councils of the Church, under Constantine the Great saw the start of a new era. The great city of Constantinople was built in which Byzantine culture was developed over many centuries. Liturgical music flourished and Syrian, and Armenian, as well as Greek, influences were felt in the new hymnody. Churchmen from the West found their way to this part of the Empire and returned home with new and vigorous ideas. Among them were St. Hilary of Poitiers, who is regarded as the earliest hymn writer of the West, and St. Ambrose of Milan. In the year 386 Ambrose was persecuted by an Emperor who subscribed to the Arian heresy, and was forced to take refuge in his church, where he was surrounded by his anxious congregation. His pupil, St. Augustine of Hippo, described the scene:

There and then it was first arranged that according to the custom of the Eastern parts, hymns and antiphons should be sung, lest the people should faint through the fatigue and sorrow; from that day to this the custom has been retained; and today many, indeed, almost all congregations throughout the parts of the world, follow our practice in this respect.

St. Ambrose composed hymns for the daily services of the Church, for special seasons of the Church's year, and for Saints' Days: thus he made Milan, for a time, the centre of the music and poetry of the Western Church, developing a tradition that rapidly grew away from that of the Eastern branch.

The nurture of art and knowledge during the next eight hundred years or so was largely the responsibility of monastic communities. The solitary life was cultivated from the earliest days of Christianity and many religious communities were established, especially in Egypt. It was, however, St. Benedict (480–540) who so organized the religious life that monasticism became an essential part of European civilization. St. Benedict, the founder of the famous Abbey of Monte Cassino in Italy, taught that monks should not only pray but also work for the common good. The Benedictines, therefore, cultivated the land, housed and cared for the sick, copied manuscripts and built libraries in which these should be preserved.

Of the many Benedictine monasteries founded in Europe during the troubled centuries that succeeded the decline of the Roman Empire none was more famous than that of St. Gall in Switzerland. The original plan of the seventh-century buildings still survives, and the great library that was first established in those far-off times contains many relics of the earliest surviving examples of Western liturgical music.

From the time of St. Benedict onwards the Christian Church was a missionary church, and the wider administration of the Church owed much to the greatest of the early Popes—St. Gregory. He was a great organizer, and imposed a general pattern of discipline on all the varied activities of the Church, including church music. The modes, or scales, which were the basis of Western music until the Renaissance, were regularized by him, and therefore carry his name. These modes, known sometimes by Greek titles, were a combination of all sorts of previous theoretical arrangements. By now the singing of liturgical music was entrusted to professional singers, and a Song School flourished in Rome. Soon singers who received their training therein were to be sent abroad to ensure that there was the same uniformity in music as in other departments of church life.

England became Christian largely through the coming

Monkwearmouth Church

of St. Augustine, who founded the see of Canterbury. The heroic days of English Christianity are described by the Venerable Bede in one of the greatest and most readable of books—*The Ecclesiastical History of the English Nation*. In the year 680 there arrived in the north of England "the Venerable John, archchanter of the church of the holy Apostle Peter". John was sent to England by order of the Pope, and he established himself in the new monastery at Monkwearmouth (now part of the town of Sunderland). The abbot, writes Bede:

then received the aforesaid Abbot John to be conducted into Britain, that he might, throughout the year, teach in his monastery the method of singing as it was practised at St. Peter's in Rome. The Abbot John did as he had been commanded by the Pope, teaching the singers of the said monastery the order and manner of singing and reading aloud, and committing to writing all that was necessary throughout the whole course of the year for the celebration of festivals; all which are still observed in that monastery; and have been copied by many others elsewhere.

The music taught by John (who stayed in England for two years) was strange and new to most of the English people, and it was some time before it became naturalized. But the institution of schools of song was a start, for when music became part of the formal organization of the Church it was regarded as one of the responsibilities of the senior clergy, who may or may not have been musical but whose administrative duties were binding.

It was, however, not easy to impose uniform standards, as was discovered in France. In the eighth century the Emperor Charlemagne, whose court was a notable centre of culture, requested twelve singers from Rome to teach his subjects the proper way of singing church music. Each singer was sent to a different part of the country. Their coming was resented by the French, for they held a high opinion of their own gifts in song. The missionary singing-teachers, finding that they could make no headway, held a conference among themselves and decided to teach not one way of singing but twelve different ones. When Charlemagne heard about this he was not pleased, and sent a message to the Pope demanding punishment for the instructors whose sense of humour was so much stronger than their sense of duty.

Gradually, however, a universal tradition of church

music became established in Western Europe. That this was so was due to the subordination of music to the liturgy, music existing not in its own right but primarily as a vehicle for words.

The principal service of the Church was the Mass, and the pattern of the Mass, not finally fixed until the eleventh century, exercised a powerful influence on music, not only in medieval but also in later times. The main parts of the liturgical Mass, known as the *Ordinary*, are the *Kyrie* (with Greek words, taken from the rites of the Eastern branch of the Church), *Gloria*, *Credo*, *Sanctus*, and *Agnus Dei*. These were, and are, invariable. For particular occasions, however, other appropriate sections are added, known as the *Proper* of the Mass. Of special forms of the Mass the most notable is that for the Dead, and this is known as the *Requiem*, the title being taken from the first word of the opening hymn. The Requiem Mass has also played an important part in Western music, and its influence has been felt outside the domain of church music.

The other services of the Church settled at an early date were the Offices or "Hours". These developed in the monastic system, and, as the name "Hours" signifies, took place at stated times throughout the day. In these services there were psalms, canticles (especially the *Magnificat*) and hymns.

All the music was, according to the ruling of St. Gregory, in "plain chant", and unaccompanied. It was basically simple, in general with one note to a syllable. Simplicity in religious music is an abiding principle, and the fundamental musical practices of all forms of worship are similar. The Gregorian type of chant is still maintained in the Roman Catholic Church. But the Anglican chant and the Calvinist psalm tune also show the supremacy of the word and a measure of austerity in the music.

It is, however, impossible to stem a natural zest for exploration. Thus the free-flowing rhapsodic instinct, apparent in all folk-music, found its place in medieval music through the hymns, of which the words were also more freely inspired. Hymns of many kinds were composed and from them grew the first religious dramas of the West. At Winchester in the tenth century there was an Easter hymn entitled *Quem quaeritis?* ("Whom do you seek?") and its manner of performance was thus described:

> While the third lesson is being chanted, one of four brethren should approach the sepulchre and sit there quietly with a palm in his hand. While the third response is chanted, three brethren should follow and, walking as those do who are looking for something, come to the sepulchre. These things are done in imitation of the angel sitting in the tomb of Jesus and the women with spices coming to anoint His body. When the brother sitting by the sepulchre sees the other three coming he should begin—in a sweet voice of medium pitch—to sing *Quem quaeritis?* When he has sung it all the three reply, in unison, *Jesu Nazarenum*.

From such sources developed the Mystery and Miracle plays, which became a colourful and popular part of the later medieval scene.

The establishment of the liturgy of the Christian Church was due not only to the zeal of missionary priests but also to the preservation of the liturgy in written form. The Mass Books, Psalters, and Hymnals of the early middle ages, which were copied and illuminated—or illustrated— by generations of monks, are among the most beautiful of works of art. In their illustrations may be seen many influences, of Celtic, Scandinavian, Byzantine, Anglo-Saxon, French, and German traditions in art; all consecrated to a common purpose. Such a wealth of artistic origins gives some idea of the growth of liturgical music, which also embraced and joined together different styles.

The establishment of musical uniformity is only possible when music is written down. As we have seen the Greeks and Egyptians, as well as the Indians and the Chinese in pre-Christian times, had some form of musical notation. In general this was alphabetic. One of the tasks of early Christian musicians was to evolve a satisfactory notation for the preservation of sacred songs.

In the second century a Byzantine scholar used a method of indicating the rise and fall of melody which was based on the accent signs of language. This system was known as neumatic, as the individual signs were called neumes. In many early manuscripts the neumes may be seen set above the words of hymns, and it can be understood how these were valuable in helping singers to remember the music they had previously learned by ear. Gradually the neumes, sometimes associated with letters of the alphabet to give more precise information, became more meaningful as their shapes became standardized to give some idea of time as well as of pitch values.

We have already heard of the famous Benedictine monastery of St. Gall in Switzerland. In the library (the present building is of the eighteenth century) are many manuscripts with neumatic musical notation. Among the famous monks of St. Gall was one, known as Notker, who died in the year 912. Because there were others of the same name he was distinguished as Notker Balbulus; the last word, meaning "stammerer", gives a curiously direct personal impression of this scholar of so long ago. Notker wrote much about music, for he was greatly interested in its theory. His contribution to our music was through an additional use of letters of the alphabet, for he showed how they could indicate expression. That old music was lacking in colour and emotional interest is disproved by Notker's indications, which included symbols for what we would now call *piano, forte, moderato, piu mosso, a tempo*, and *sforzando*. Singers of the tenth century clearly took pleasure in their duties.

Another monk of the tenth century in whose debt we are was the Flemish Hucbald. He was a historian, a poet, an educational administrator, and a student of music. As in Platonic times music was studied less by specialists than by general scholars who treated music as a part of a unified philosophic system. Hucbald, considering musical notation as it was in his day, saw that neumes were unsatisfactory as a means of guiding the voice because they gave no absolute idea of pitch or interval. Therefore he introduced lines, representing perhaps the strings or keys of an instrument, between which the neumes should be set. Here, then, is the beginning of the staff notation.

A hundred years later a further advance was made by the Italian Benedictine monk Guido, of Arezzo. Guido travelled widely, in France, in Germany, possibly in England, as well as in Italy. He was a practical musician and not merely a theorist, and his writings about music were valuable on this account. Guido, no doubt developing ideas he had noted in his travels, established the sol-fa system, the precise stave, and also hand-signs as a means of teaching pitch relationships.

Sol-fa was based on syllables found in a medieval hymn and they were as follows: *Ut* (now called *doh*), *re, mi, fa, sol, la. Te* belongs to more modern times, for Guido and his contemporaries thought in terms of the six-note, or hexachordal, arrangement of sounds. The sol-fa names thus established were of immense value in encouraging correctness in the singing of intervals. Accuracy was further ensured by more definition in written music. Hucbald had introduced lines. Guido spaced these lines exactly and gave to each a particular pitch significance. Thus a red line stood for the sound otherwise described in alphabetic notation as F, a yellow line for C, a green line for B flat. Any other lines required were drawn in black.

Another worker in this field whose name deserves commemoration was the writer of the eleventh or twelfth century known as Franco of Cologne. He modified the shapes of the neumes so that their time-value might be generally understood.

So much having been accomplished, over many centuries, in regard to musical notation, the composition of

Anglo-Saxon gleemen, from an eighth-century English Psalter

music otherwise than by extempore means appears as a possible activity. But this was not feasible until there was some relaxation of the theoretical controls that narrowed serious music—that is church music—to the limits of unaccompanied chant.

The Christian Fathers, influenced particularly by St. Augustine of Hippo, were firm in rejecting instrumental music in church. For nearly a thousand years, then, European music as a whole was hindered by the cultivation of one sort of music, under scholarly guidance, in the cloister, and another—folk-song and dance—without. The division between "serious" and "light" music is by no means peculiar to our own day.

The churchmen, however, were not ignorant of instrumental music. St. Gregory himself found the psaltery, the drum, the trumpet, and the cithara useful for illustrating points of theology in his sermons, while the illustrators of the Utrecht Psalter of the tenth century, as well as those of other manuscripts, showed many instrumental groups in action.

Instruments of the harp type were, as we have seen, in use at an early date. The British harp of the seventh century—one especially associated with bards—was called the *cruit*, or *crot*, and its use is described by the hymn-writer Venantius of Poitiers. The Irish version of the cruit is illustrated in the sculptures of some of the High Crosses of the eighth and ninth centuries. The word crot changed into rote, and this word is to be found in medieval English literature. The *psaltery*, to which St. Gregory referred, was also a stringed instrument, in which strings, set across a frame and tuned by tuning pins, were vibrated either by the fingers or by a plectrum. By the eleventh century the principle of bowing strings was well established in Britain. The earliest specimen of an instrument

Anglo-Saxon gleemen, from a medieval Psalter, c. 1050

approximating to a violin belongs to the eleventh century, for an Anglo-Saxon Psalter of that date shows one in the hands of the Welsh saint Asaph. This instrument was known as a *crowd*.

Pipes similar to those used by the Romans and the Greeks appear in many manuscripts and sculptures, and on the Irish High Crosses of Monasterboice and Clonmacnoise, erected during the tenth century, are shown both double and single pipes. The Utrecht Psalter illustrates wind instruments made from the horns of animals, pan-pipes and clappers. But what particularly catches the eye is a picture of an organ, with four attendants anxiously

43

maintaining the wind supply under the agitated gaze of two players at each end of the row of pipes.

The organ went into exile some time about the fourth century. Its reappearance several hundred years later was due once again to the interaction of one culture on another. Organs were not favoured in Western Europe; but they continued to keep their place in Byzantine music. At the beginning of the eighth century the organ was known in Anglo-Saxon England, but its use as an accompaniment to sacred music was first officially urged by the Emperor Pepin, father of Charlemagne. As the organ was quite unknown in France or Germany he sent a request to the Byzantine Emperor that such an instrument might be sent from Constantinople. The first organ was set up in the church in Compiègne, and in 812 a copy was installed in Aachen. Thereafter the organ enjoyed great popularity in France and Germany, and German organ-makers soon became famous. The earliest German organs were in the modern province of Saxony, the land of Handel and Bach, especially at Erfurt and Magdeburg.

St. Dunstan, who was a very practical saint—being notable in the arts of metal-work, painting, and literature —was an enthusiastic designer of organs in England, erecting instruments in the abbeys of Malmesbury and Abingdon. The most famous English organ, however, was that installed in Winchester Cathedral at the order of Bishop Elphege in the middle of the tenth century. This organ was celebrated by the poet Wulstan, who was one of the priests at Winchester.

This instrument had four hundred pipes arranged in sets of ten. To each row of ten pipes was a slider by which wind was admitted to the pipes. The forty slides were controlled by two players, and on each slider was inscribed its alphabetical name. The wind came from twenty-six bellows which were worked, said Wulstan, by seventy strong men. He does not omit to mention that so hard did they have to work that they were covered in perspiration. As to the effect of the organ:

> the iron sounds beat on the ear like thunder, and they carry in every direction. None can come near to the sounds of this organ and every one stops his ears with his hands. The music is heard throughout the whole town. . . .

It is clear that in Anglo-Saxon times the air was alive with different sorts of music. The next step was the bringing together of these strains.

3

Medieval Music

U P to the time of the Norman conquest of England the
peoples of Europe were concerned with the recon-
struction of the various units of society from the ruins of
the formerly powerful Empire of Rome. What was left of
that imperialism remained in the attitude and government of the Church, which imposed some sort of uniformity in doctrine and in organization through the medium of
Latin. As has been seen there was within the Church some
scope for originality of expression at least through the
visual arts, in which many regional characteristics were to
be found. Such deviation was less easy in music, because
of the lack of a means whereby original ideas could be
adequately represented in written form, and because of
the tight hold kept on music by ecclesiastical authority.

Any organization, whether secular or religious, tends
towards a conservative (i.e. conserving) point of view in
respect of the arts; for by drawing attention to tradition
and by emphasizing its virtues the organization implies its
own durability and power. The story of church music in
the medieval period is that of those who did not wish for
any change in fundamentals and those who did; between
those who were suspicious of new ideas and those who welcomed them.

During that period church music also began to lose its
privileged position. Nations arose under the leadership of

strong kings, round whom developed court rituals and traditions in which music played an important part. Nominally Church and State were one, and medieval Christian monarchs did not appear deliberately to usurp the artistic property of the Church; but royal music stood out more and more in contrast to sacred music. Gradually

Bagpiper, Beverley Minster, Yorkshire, c. 1325

it made contact with the music of the people, and this fusion ultimately led to the enrichment of music as an art.

Between the eleventh and the fifteenth centuries most of the great cathedral churches of Europe were built. The Romanesque style was succeeded by the more fluent Gothic, and each city of importance was dominated by the clustered spires that symbolized authority and aspiration. Within the churches windows were filled with brilliant stained glass, such as remains at Chartres or at York; the walls were covered with mural paintings that gave both delight and instruction; sculpture, both in wood and in stone, further indicated a new confidence and zest for living. Such developments were partly the result of a more extensive ceremonial, and partly of a realization of their educational value, but they also derived from a more or less independently enlarged technical capacity.

Plainsong, the official music of the Church, was in theory simple, unaccompanied, and in unison. By the tenth century, however, accompaniment was possible, even though the organ often did no more than duplicate the notes of the singers. The great organ at Winchester provided a more ambitious effect, for the rows of pipes operated by the sliders let out simultaneously with the melody notes other notes at a distance of fifth and octave. As a melody proceeded, then, the organ drew a series of parallel tunes.

But the singers themselves were also doing this. Unison singing breaks down when some singers find that certain parts of a melody are too high or too low for comfort. At this point the individual singer sensibly transposes the melody to a more acceptable compass. This is to be found in all early musical culture and the parallel part singing which began to be a regular feature of European church music about the tenth century is also to be found in active folk-music.

Aachen

This form of parallel singing was known as *organum*. By the eleventh century organum was modified so that sometimes there was contrary movement of the parts, the one going up while the other went down. Still the basis of music was the traditional plain-chant melody, even though either one or two extra parts might be added above or below.

The development of music depended on the trained musicians attached to the cathedral and monastic foundations. In the twelfth and thirteenth centuries one of the most important schools of music was in Paris, at Notre Dame. The director of music there in the twelfth century was Leoninus, and eighty of his compositions have survived. These are *organa*, eighty in all, composed for the major feasts of the church. In some of his organa Leoninus

Notre Dame, Paris

gives the main melody in very long notes above which a second voice descants freely in much quicker notes. In others the two parts move, note by note, in the same rhythm. In this case the rhythm is often derived from the secular songs of the troubadours.

After Leoninus came Perotinus, in whose works can be seen the earliest examples of motets. The essence of a motet is that it allowed other words than those given in the fundamental plain chant.

Music in three and four parts, such as is shown in some of the works of Perotinus, necessitates consideration of two factors. One is rhythm; and during the thirteenth century the character of notes of different lengths and their relationship to one another, through their division in two or three parts, was defined. The other factor is that which we

Norman capital, crypt of St. Gabriel, Canterbury Cathedral, c. 1120

now call harmonic. As soon as the major and the minor chord were accepted as points of repose in the texture of music harmony was born. By the end of the thirteenth century this term was in use (not in its modern restricted sense but as an agreed definition of part-music) in the writings of an English west-country scholar, Walter of Oddington.

As we look back across the centuries the next progress of music from single-line melody to more or less complex works in three or four parts seems inevitable. But there were at all times powerful critics. The conservative point of view was forcefully expressed at the beginning of the fourteenth century by the eighty-year-old Pope John XXII. He issued a long decree from Avignon in 1322 in which he complained of those who preferred to devise methods of their own rather than to continue singing in the old tradition and of those who set secular songs against sacred melodies in their motets. He feared that the Gregorian modes would be forgotten and that the chants in the Antiphonal and Gradual books would be altered out of all recognition. He gave a modified approval, however, to certain harmonies which might be expected "to soothe the hearer and arouse his devotion". Anyone who disobeyed Papal instructions was to be suspended from office.

Such an attempt to control music was no new thing in the Middle Ages; nor is the idea, that music should be controlled by non-musicians, dead in our own day.

In the Middle Ages the office of kingship was generally regarded (despite the manner in which some kings obtained their crowns) as of divine ordinance. This idea was helped somewhat by the singing of suitable "royal" music. King John was frequently accompanied on his travels by a small number of servants whose primary duty was to sing the royal hymn *Christus vincit*. These servants were known as clerks and they held office under the Chancellor in the Chapel Royal.

Between the twelfth and fifteenth centuries the Chapel Royal, especially in France and in England, played an important part in the development of music. The Chapel, with its singers, travelled with the King wherever he went and if, as was frequent with English kings, such journeys were to France, then the musicians were able to exchange ideas with their counterparts abroad.

In the reign of Edward I an inventory was made of the possessions of the Chapel Royal, and in it were described two books of organa, which had either been imported from France, or copied from French books. During the same reign we find that choirboys of the Chapel, their voices having broken, were sent to Oxford at the King's expense. Study in the schools there would ultimately fit them for office as clerks, and from that time on many choristers of the King grew up to be officers of the Crown in later life. A number were to become composers.

The special cultivation of sacred music at court was a sign of rising interest in more civilized qualities in life. Kings and their attendant barons and officers might still be hard, ruthless, cruel men; but they recognized that some common cultural standards helped in uniting action with thought and ideal.

A striking feature of medieval thought was a chivalrous devotion to women, who—in theory, at least, and in the highest social groups—enjoyed more polite attention than at any other time in European history. Again this partly stemmed from theology, from the cult of the Virgin Mary, to whom many shrines and churches were dedicated, and in whose honour many hymns were composed.

Court life, with its pleasures, encouraged attention to the beauties there assembled, and the invention of suitable

53

poems and songs for their flattery became a prosperous industry. The pioneers of this cult were to be found in France, the land of troubadours and *trouvères* (the former based in the south, the latter in the north). Courtiers kept their hopes of feminine companionship bright by their skill in composition and performance. Naturally they were not all talented artists, and often needed professional advice and assistance. This is where the popular minstrels, outside the jurisdiction of the Church, came into their own; for the clergy could hardly be expected to lend much aid—unless, perhaps, unofficially.

Between them the troubadours, trouvères and minstrels laid the foundations of secular song and musical form. There were different kinds of songs. Some were proper to Crusaders—for the troubadour art flourished in the time of the Crusades; some were memorials to knights who had died in the wars; some were designed for competitions, like that described in Wagner's opera *Tannhäuser*; some were of a pastoral character; but the great majority were in praise of beauty and of love. Some songs were similar in pattern to hymns, with the same melody for each verse; some were constructed in simpler plainsong manner, with the same melody repeated for each line of poetry; some borrowed from dance forms and of them the most celebrated was the *carol*, from which came the characteristic *rondeau* with alternation between soloist and chorus.

Many of the medieval secular songs were written down, in the same notation as was employed in church music. They were often in the scales or modes of the Church, but sometimes in what in later times came to be known as the major scale. No accompaniments, however, were preserved, for these were extemporized on the indispensable lute.

In the twelfth and thirteenth centuries the greatest

*Masked mummers, from the MS. of the Roman de Fauvel,
fourteenth century*

patrons of the art of secular song were William, Count of
Poitiers, and Thibaut de Champagne, King of Navarre.

The French example spread, and music of the troubadour order was practised in England (especially in the
time of Richard I) and in Germany. In that country the
art of the troubadours developed into that of the *Minnesänger* (literally, "love" singers), and the most famous of
the *Minnesänger* were Walther von der Vogelweide and
Wolfram von Eschenbach.

Walther von der Vogelweide was typical of many
medieval minstrels and bards in that he travelled from
court to court. At one time he was under the patronage of
Hermann of Thuringia, at another of Philip of Swabia, at
another of Dietrich of Meissen. Walther was a sturdy
and independent character and gained both respect and

disapproval for supporting the Emperor against the Pope; in the privileged position enjoyed by medieval secular musicians he was therefore beginning to sow the seeds of discord between Church and State that came to fruition centuries later. Wolfram, a Bavarian who was also in service at the Thuringian Court, adapted a French tale and presented it in German form under the title of *Parzival*. Six centuries later this popular legend of the Middle Ages was read by Richard Wagner, who was thus inspired to compose his music drama on the same subject.

By the thirteenth century there was much more connection between the sacred and secular in music than the more rigorous and conservative of the churchmen would have readily acknowledged. The development of rhythmic part-singing in church was, as we have seen from the music of Perotinus, assisted by troubadour practice. The most attractive and familiar music to show the union of "serious" and "light" is "Summer is i-cumen in", which was written

King David playing bells, from the St. Omer Psalter, fifteenth century

56

at Reading Abbey in the thirteenth century. The melody is popular in style; its treatment in canon, above the two-part refrain of the lower voices, displays the mastery of the monastic, academic composer experienced in composing in parts. The English words are lively and secular, but there is an alternative and sober set of Latin verses which make a hymn.

The connection between the tradition of the Church and the new secular tradition of the court was an emancipating influence in music; for music, together with poetry, now became recognized in its own right and with its own values. But there were often fertilizing influences. Provençal poetry, from which sprang all troubadour art, was at first inspired by Arabic models. Instruments of the lute family were introduced to Europe from Persian, Arabic and Moorish sources through the Moors in Spain and the Saracens in Sicily and Southern Italy. From the Islamic world of the Middle East, visited by so many Crusaders, came other instruments, including oboes and kettle-drums. And in each country of Europe a fresh vitality was arising from the growing skill and political awareness of the mass of the people.

Away from capital cities, the seats of princes, and the rich abbeys, medieval people lived hard and anxious lives; most of them in varying degrees of serfdom. Their main preoccupation was with food and shelter; they lived constantly under the threat of plague, famine, and war; and rarely were they able to travel further than the end of their villages. Music then was a necessity, a release from the bondage of everyday drudgery. This was often the case also in later times and under a different sort of tyranny—especially that imposed by the Industrial Revolution.

In the eleventh and twelfth centuries the ceremonial of

Angel trumpeter, stained glass, Sainte Chapelle, Paris,
fifteenth century

the Church was in many places enriched by an increasing repertoire of religious dramas with music. The subjects of these primitive plays were those which attracted oratorio composers of later time, and among them were the stories of the Nativity and the Resurrection, of the wise and foolish virgins, of Daniel and Belshazzar, and of St. Nicholas. These performances were particularly popular in France and Germany. Some of the plays about St. Nicholas were written by Hilarius, a pupil of the Parisian monk-philosopher, Abelard.

Hilarius was one of a group of poets known as Goliards (the name taken from a reputed Bishop Golias). These were students, usually of modest origin, who decided not to proceed with the careers open to them in the Church, the only "safe" careers in those times, but to trade their imagination and their talent in letters and drama—as did the minstrels and jugglers and acrobats theirs—wherever they were welcome. Life being as it was they generally were welcome, for they brought fresh interest to isolated communities, and news of the outside world. Sometimes the plays of the Goliards were in the repertory of travelling groups of players, who were engaged to perform even in monasteries.

The most famous poems of the Goliards, rough and robust, were the collections of *Carmina Burana*—with neumes in the original manuscripts—which are of present interest in that they inspired a striking work of the twentieth century by the German composer Carl Orff.

Minstrels, together with the other entertainers with whom they were generally grouped, were a mixed class. Some were attracted to manorial and princely households. Such was Melioso, the harp player employed by Sir John Matravers. When King Edward I visited Sir John he was taken ill and had to be bled. As the operation was in progress Melioso soothed the monarch's nerves by harp music, for which he was rewarded with a gift—a truly princely gift—of 20 shillings. For the most part, however, minstrels were wanderers and generally under severe criticism by the Church. This criticism was founded on a righteous distaste for the doubtful moral quality of much of their entertainment, and also on their frequent rejection of the clerical careers for which they had been destined. There was another point: the minstrels were able to influence opinion and when they criticized and satirized the rules, whether religious or secular, their words were an effective spur to discontent.

Harpist: arch moulding of doorway, Barfreston Church, Kent,
twelfth century

At the beginning of the fourteenth century the minstrels
began to band themselves together, as in a union, and the
earliest guild which sought to protect the minstrels'
interests and to guarantee their skill was the *Corporation des
Menestrels* in Paris. Soon afterwards similar bodies were
established in other countries.

There are a few men in every age who impress their

influence not only on their contemporaries but also on posterity, not only on their own country but universally. In the thirteenth century such a man was St. Francis of Assisi. By his life, and through the Order of Friars which carried his ideas and ideals far and wide, St. Francis gave a new dignity to human personality. He broke down barriers between class and class; he taught men thankfully to employ what was beautiful; and he encouraged a faith in individual achievement. Through St. Francis the arts took a new lease of life.

St. Francis, however, was fortunate in belonging to the Republic of Florence, which was the greatest political power in Italy and also the most notable centre of artistic achievement. Church music flourished on the one hand and the art of the troubadours on the other, while the peasants of Tuscany united secular and sacred in their own way in the songs they sang during the processions organized in honour of the great Festivals of the Church. St. Francis combined the best of these traditions and practices in his *Lauds*, or hymns, and the succeeding Franciscans captivated hearers in all lands by their new songs. The influence of St. Francis and the Franciscans is also reflected in the new style of painting particular to Florence in the thirteenth century. The life story of the great saint inspired Cimabue and his more famous disciple Giotto. Giotto's painting showed action, which was not characteristic of the previous prevailing Byzantine idiom, and he was the first to show landscape in his backgrounds. The meeting of sacred and secular elements in his art was akin to that in the songs of the same period. In Italy especially, from that time and through the Renaissance, music and painting were closely allied.

Both these arts, however, were also associated with literature, and another great name in Florentine history must now make its entry: that of the poet and philosopher Dante, who was the friend of Giotto.

Dante, who was devoted to music in his youth according to his biographer Boccaccio, was the founder of the Italian language through his refinement of what previously had been the Tuscan dialect. He was also always alive to the possibilities inherent in the fusion of words and melody. Many musicians were among his friends, and often—says Boccaccio—he "composed poems, which he caused musicians to clothe in pleasing and masterly melody". In the second book of his *Divine Comedy* Dante introduces us to one of the song-writers of thirteenth-century Florence. The scene is in Purgatory, and Dante sees a shadowy form dart forward to greet him. Until he hears the voice he is not sure who it is, but by the voice he recalls his old friend, Pietro Casella. Casella had set many of Dante's poems to music and now Dante asks him to sing one of them again:

> If new law taketh not from thee
> Memory or custom of love-tuned song,
> That whilom all my cares had power to assuage;
> Please thee therewith a little to console
> My spirit, that encumbered with its frame,
> Travelling so far, of pain is overcome.
> "Love, that discourses in my thoughts," he then
> Began in such soft accents, that within
> The sweetness thrills me yet. My gentle guide,
> And all who came with him, so well were pleased,
> That seemed naught else might in their thoughts
>   have room.

Dante makes many references to music in the *Divine Comedy*, from which we may build a fairly detailed picture of its place in thirteenth-century Italian life. Many familiar hymns are mentioned, including the *Sanctus* and *Hosanna* of the Mass; the *Te Deum laudamus*—traditionally ascribed to St. Ambrose of Milan; the evening hymn *Te lucis ante*, known in its English form as "Before the ending of the day"; the popular twelfth-century devotions to Mary entitled *Salve Regina* and *Regina Coeli*. The most interesting reference, however, is to *Vexilla regis* ("The banners of the King"), a hymn composed in the sixth century in honour of the presentation of "relics of the True Cross" by Queen Rhadegund to the monastery at Poitiers. In the last part of the first Book of the *Divine Comedy*, in which the poet imagines himself in Hell, Dante gives a parody of the hymn:

> The banners of Hell's Monarch do come forth
> Towards us.

All these quotations should be seen in their contexts, which show what effect the music of the Church had on sensitive ears; but it represented jubilation, sadness, repentance, and so on. Dante's feelings in this respect were romantic, and it is apparent that poetry and music in divine worship exercised a greater influence than was allowed by purely theoretical writers.

Famous troubadours are mentioned by Dante. In *Hell* Dante encountered Bertrand de Born, who was, said Dante in another work, the first poet of that period to make war a subject of verse. A second, found in *Purgatory*, was Arnaut Daniel, who worked both in England—at the court of Richard I—and in Italy. Also in *Purgatory* there is mention of "the songster of Limoges", Giraud de Borneil. Yet another secular musician was one Belacqua. A marginal note in the copy of Dante's poem in the Monastery of Monte Cassino describes him as "an excellent master of the harp and lute, but very negligent in his affairs both spiritual and temporal". Therefore, perhaps, he was placed by Dante in *Purgatory*.

The principal instruments in use during his day are also mentioned by Dante: the trumpets, drums and bells that "give only the notes of war"; the organ as it mingles with the broad strains of the *Te Deum*; and the popular harp, cittern, lyre, lute, shepherd's pipe (in various forms), and cornet. More and more these instruments came into play in the next period, which may be inaugurated by the poet Boccaccio and the composer Landino, who were also citizens of Florence.

4

Parting of the Ways

ONE of the great works of fourteenth-century Italian
literature is the *Decameron*, by Boccaccio. In 1348
Florence was visited by the plague, and many people
escaped from the stricken city into the surrounding
countryside. Among them was a group of young people,
seven girls and three young men, who found sanctuary in
a beautiful villa in the hills. There they whiled away the
time by telling each other stories (which are recounted by
Boccaccio), and by taking part in musical performances:

> Dioneo took a lute and Fiametta a viol and they began
> softly to play a dance; then Parmeno (the "queen" of the
> group) and the other ladies, together with the other two
> young men, struck up a round and began with a slow pace
> to dance a brawl. When that was ended they sang curious
> and amusing songs.

From this we learn that the lute was a man's instrument
in Florence while well-bred ladies played the viol, and
that dances were by now played in two parts—this is also
mentioned by Dante as well as other contemporary
writers. Among these other writers was Giovanni de Prato,
who describes a similar upper-middle-class party to that of
Boccaccio's; but he introduces to the guests a real composer, Francesco Landino, one of the most celebrated
characters of fourteenth-century Florence.

E   65

Landino was the son of a painter. In childhood he became blind as a consequence of smallpox, but this misfortune only quickened his determination to excel in music. He studied deeply, and not only in music, for he was renowned for his acquaintance with literature and philosophy. In middle life, indeed, he was crowned with a laurel wreath in Venice as the winner of a contest in poetry. It was, however, as organist that Landino was most famous, and his tombstone, in the church of St.

Francesco Landino playing a portable organ,
from a fourteenth-century MS.

Lorenzo in Florence, shows him holding a small portative (movable) organ in his hand. Like all musicians of older times he was proficient on other instruments and played the lute, the rebec (a bowed instrument of Eastern origin), and the recorder. Above all these accomplishments Landino was a composer; perhaps the first distinctive composer of the Italian tradition, and certainly one of the fathers of Italian music.

Landino's music grew from the cultural climate of Florentine society, and his works would have fitted admirably into the scenes described by Boccaccio. He composed many dance songs and ballads (the Italian ballad was different in form from the French) as well as *caccias* (part songs of a popular order based on realistic episodes in country life) and madrigals. This introduces a word made much more familiar two centuries later. The fourteenth-century madrigal was quite different in style from its successor, consisting generally of several stanzas sung to the same melody and completed by a refrain somewhat similar to the *envoi* of the poetic ballad of Chaucer. The melody was supported by one or two other voices and key instruments. Twelve of Landino's madrigals have survived.

Because Florence was an important political and commercial city it was visited frequently by foreigners. One of the most important visitors of the later fourteenth century was Geoffrey Chaucer, whose *Canterbury Tales* owed much to the influence of the great writers of Florence. Chaucer, however, was also well acquainted with France, where he had been, at different times, both a prisoner of war and a diplomat. If in Florence he had heard of Landino in Paris he certainly would have heard of the great French composer Guillaume de Machaut. It has, indeed, been suggested that Chaucer was directly influenced by Machaut's poetry.

Like Landino, Machaut was a man of many parts. He was born of humble parentage, but was educated at the university and took clerical orders. His general ability was considerable, and he became a court official, serving in turn the King of Bohemia, the Duchess of Normandy, the King of Navarre, and the King of France. In later life he settled in Rheims as a canon of the cathedral, there devoting himself to sacred music.

Machaut wrote poems, mostly after the manner of the *trouvères*, and immediately set them to music. Some pieces, especially those termed *lais* and *virelais*, were for the voice only, but many *motets* (secular motets, that is), *rondeaux*, and *virelais* were for two or three voices with frequent accompanying instrumental parts. Of Machaut's church music the most important example is the Mass for four voices that is thought to have been composed for the coronation of King Charles V at Rheims in 1364. This is the earliest Mass for a number of voices, termed polyphonic, known to be the work of a particular composer.

The fourteenth century was an age of increasing travel, so far as the upper classes were concerned, and musicians were often fortunate in their patrons. Machaut, as has been seen, travelled for other reasons, but his music was universally respected, and such was his reputation that copies were made for use in Spain, Poland, and Cyprus.

The musical interests of the less conspicuous members of society in the fourteenth century are shown by Geoffrey Chaucer, who more than any writer of his age depicted the more modest classes with sympathy, tolerance, and unfailing humour. The company of pilgrims which set out for Canterbury on its immortal pilgrimage contained a rare lot of performers. The skill with which Chaucer details their various aptitudes is no small factor in bringing them to life, for we can almost hear them.

Among the singers were the Prioress, who "entuned in her nose full swetely"; the carpenter's wife, as loud and lively in song as "any swallow chittering on a barn"; the Wife of Bath, who recalled the singing of her young days which she immodestly likened to that of the nightingale; the parish clerk was both singer and actor, and used to take the part of King Herod in the mystery plays that were becoming increasingly popular; the Pardoner and the Summoner, by their clerical training more or less expert in church music, who were equally adept at singing such popular songs as "Come hither, love, to me" in two parts —the Summoner being responsible for a resonant bass.

The Friar could play the flute. So too could the young

Miller playing the bagpipes, from a fourteenth-century MS.

squire, who was something of a gallant after the French or Italian fashion, for he could also compose songs, fence, dance, paint, and write. In the *Miller's Tale* a clerk of Oxford possessed a psaltery—an instrument from which the pianoforte of later times was to develop; while other favourite instruments were the organ (Chaucer describes the organ as "merry", a description also applied to it in the carol "The Holly and the Ivy"), the harp, and—also stringed instruments—the rubible and the gittern.

At one point in the *Prioress's Tale*, Chaucer gives a glimpse of a choir school, as when the seven-year-old boy who is the sad hero of that story listens eagerly to his more practised companions as they sing the hymn *Alma Redemptoris*.

Not only literature and the few written musical remains of the period, but also sculpture, in many great churches of Europe, suggest how generally music was practised, and that towards the end of the Middle Ages the division between sacred and secular styles was much more slight than formerly; so it was also in architecture, for the same idioms served happily in church and manor. Nevertheless the intellectual development of music was still primarily a matter for the musicians employed by the Church. They had opportunities denied to others, principal among them being access to a trained and professional group of performers. To the schools of Paris and Rheims should be added that of Worcester, for in the great Benedictine monastery (now cathedral) set on the banks of the Severn was composed some of the most splendid English music of the fourteenth century. This music differs from Continental music of the same period in its conservative character and in a more mellow, harmonic quality.

Gothic thought in its later stages is distinguished by complexity, and scholars were adept at setting problems which often appeared to be ends in themselves. The intellectual possibilities inherent in musical nature and design had always attracted philosophers. By the end of the fourteenth century composers had technical means at their disposal to enable them to bring musical composition into the general intellectual field.

One of the foremost masters in Europe was the Englishman John Dunstable, a mathematician and astronomer as well as composer, who went to France in early life (in the service of the Duke of Bedford, who was Regent of France) and thereafter worked on the Continent. Dunstable was a master of choral writing, and his works—masses, motets, and antiphons—are of a scale and variety previously unknown. His influence was considerable, not least of all at the Burgundian court of Duke Philip the Good, which provided two great composers in Guillaume Dufay and Gilles Binchois.

For more than a hundred years French and Flemish composers took the lead in European music. This proposes a question. Why were the Flemings thus distinguished at one time and not at another? From which arises a second question. Are some nations more musical than others? In the answer to the first question lies also that to the second.

In the late Middle Ages the great cities of Flanders enjoyed a prosperity unparalleled in later times. They were great commercial and financial centres, and were endowed by rich merchants who expressed their pride in terms of art—as also was the case in Florence. Therefore churches and public buildings were built; artists of the calibre of Memling and the Van Eycks were engaged to adorn them, and musicians to give additional splendour. Both the artists and musicians were also encouraged to domesticate their talents, in portraits on the one hand, and *chansons* on the other.

71

The high standard of church music in the northern countries of Europe was regarded enviously in Rome, which successive Popes from the reign of the vigorous fifteenth-century Nicholas V were determined to establish as the commanding force in all branches of religious art. This followed the long arguments about the seat of the Papacy between the French and the Italians, the establishment of Popes at Avignon, and their final return to Rome. Guillaume Dufay was persuaded to Rome for a number of years, and after him went many singers and composers (the singers were composers, and the composers singers) from the Netherlands. The union was a fruitful one. Flemish music was intellectual; Italian music was sensuous; the blend of both produced a balanced style of compelling quality and universal significance.

Dufay was educated as a choirboy at the cathedral school of Cambrai. At the age of twenty-eight he joined the Papal choir, which then comprised but nine singers; next he went to Paris, and finally back to Cambrai, where he ended his days as a canon of the Cathedral Chapter. Dufay was a master of counterpoint, his music being a pattern of separate melodies weaving their way in and out of each other, often in canonic form, and always based on complicated and fascinating rhythmic figures.

From the earliest times the focal point of church music had been plainsong. In the fifteenth century the more spacious manner of composition still centred on plainsong themes, generally established in long notes in the tenor part. Sometimes, however, a secular melody replaced the plainsong. Although Dufay wrote some secular music his most important works were for the church. Binchois, on the other hand, was primarily a composer of rondeaux, ballads, and chansons. By training he was a soldier, but later became a singer in the court chapel of Philip of Burgundy.

Among Dufay's pupils was Jan Ockeghem, who had been a choirboy in the cathedral at Antwerp. Ockeghem extended the principles of his master, and the way in which his music was laid out anticipated later practice. His melodic phrases were longer. There was less dependence on a given melody—either plainsong or secular—and, therefore, more individuality in the part-writing. Up to the time of Dufay most vocal music had been set for three voices—from tenor upwards. In the second half of the fifteenth century the bass, or lowest, part came into its own.

Exploitation of the lower ranges of music affected the design of organs which, in northern Europe but not in England, began to use pedals operating pipes of 16 feet (or double-bass range) pitch.

Ockeghem added what we might now term a Romantic impulse to music, for his settings of sacred works are not only a vehicle for the words but also an extension of their significance. In this the composer was aided by a freer general treatment of the modes (chromatic notes outside the strict limits of the modes now being employed) and by a firmer sense of harmony.

Ockeghem was one notable Flemish composer of the later fifteenth century. Others were Jacob Obrecht, a native of Utrecht and sometime director of music to the Duke of Ferrara; and Josquin des Prés, who was himself a pupil of Ockeghem. Josquin des Prés, after a period in Paris, followed numerous of his compatriots to Italy, where he sang in, and composed for, choirs in Milan, Rome, Modena, and Ferrara. His influence and that of other Flemish musicians on the Italians will be described later; but now let us look back at the state of affairs in England and other countries of Europe.

By the fifteenth century England was conscious of her

73

nationhood. This was due to geography—to being an island, to the French wars which persisted from 1337 to 1453, and to the concentration of power in one centre and under the governance of kings strong enough to establish control and also to obtain for themselves some degree of personal popularity. Henry V was one of the most successful rulers of his age, and this is partly reflected in the reputation, much encouraged by their sovereign, which his Chapel Royal musicians enjoyed. When Henry V made his will he remembered his choristers, leaving £200 to be divided amongst them.

The Masters and Deans of the Chapel Royal were intent that the choir should be the best of its kind, and they obtained permission to conscript singing-boys. In the years after the battle of Agincourt in 1415, indeed, a boy with a good voice was liable to be taken away from his home and whisked off to France, where the choir was almost permanently stationed. At that time there were sixteen members of the choir, which was a relatively large number for those days.

Experience in France was invaluable for composers. Music by the king's composers—and even possibly by the king himself—is contained in a valuable manuscript, containing motets and movements from masses, known as the Old Hall Manuscript. This is now preserved in St. Edmund's College, Ware. Music of the late fifteenth century, as sung in the Chapel Royal, is preserved in another famous manuscript—the Eton Choirbook, which is the property of Eton College and of which many of the works have been lately edited and published. One of the composers represented was Gilbert Banaster, who was appointed Master of the Children of the Chapel Royal in 1474.

Musicians of those days were not narrow specialists, and

Banaster—as also some of his successors—won fame also as a poet. He was also required to arrange entertainments of a secular nature for the king's pleasure; thus he composed some secular songs.

The rise in esteem of secular music is indicated in the English (as also in the French) court records. Trumpeters, pipers, drummers, and other players became a regular part of the royal household. When he went to France Henry V took fifteen such musicians with him, under the control of one Walter Holiday. Holiday worked on through the reigns of Henry VI and Edward IV, from whom he received a charter giving the royal minstrels a regular status and constitution. They were, as a body,

Entry of Louis XII into Paris, 1498, from a woodcut

subject to the orders of the marshal and two wardens elected from their number.

In the fifteenth century the institution of monarchy became increasingly invested with symbolism. The personality of the monarch was projected through the magic of spectacle, poetry, and music. Masquerades, ballets, tournaments, and "triumphs" were developed from folk-customs on the one hand and courtly and even ecclesiastical art on the other. In Italy, at the court of Philip of Burgundy, and in England especially, much money was lavished on gorgeous displays.

When King Henry VI returned to England from France in 1431 the city of London greeted him with a pageant which was spread over the main thoroughfares. Choristers appeared in fancy dress to sing welcome songs "with a heavenly melody", and at St. Paul's Gate was set up a large representation of the Holy Trinity, surrounded by minstrels disguised as archangels "playing and singing upon all instruments of music". Among the poets called in to provide texts for royal entertainments was John Lydgate, who dragged in references from both scripture and classical mythology to flatter his king and queen.

Just as these secular displays invaded religious territory, so did the sacred drama of mystery and miracle play encroach on the worldly. The plays which were performed on the great festivals of the Church (which also were public holidays) in the larger English cities were taken from one point to another in the towns on wagons, or "pageants", and audiences were enchanted by the tunefulness of the music, by the comedy of the shepherds of the Nativity, and by the blood-curdling acts of King Herod, as much as they were instructed in the deeper significance of the faith.

The ancient courtly art of the troubadour was dead in the fifteenth century, but its traditions were absorbed into the larger art forms of the period. In Germany the last of the *Minnesänger* died in 1445, but there the tradition was transformed into the middle-class art of the *Meistersinger*. The great German cities of

Reinmar the Elder, Minnesänger, from an illuminated manuscript

the late Middle Ages were sturdily independent and controlled in large measure by the burghers themselves. Music played its part in civic life in a characteristic way. The bands of town musicians were well organized and frequently in demand for public performances. Often the wind instruments would play from the balconies of the town halls or, more strikingly, from the high towers of the Gothic churches—a tradition maintained in some cities to this day.

Under the control of the *Meistersinger* music for the middle classes became a serious affair. Rules were drawn up regarding composition and performance, and many contests were held. The melodies of the *Meistersinger* were derived from folk-song and the music of the Church and in due course this music was to play a part in the political and religious upheavals of the sixteenth century. The half-century before the Reformation was indeed an important time in German music, for during that period it became democratic in impulse, and song was fashioned as a medium for transmitting simple and powerful aspects of personal and communal belief. The direct rhythmic melodies which were collected in the song-books of Bavaria and Swabia and Saxony in the fifteenth century are still sung with fervour in present-day Germany.

No religious movement has ever lacked musical expression. In the late fifteenth century the music of the Roman Church was approaching one of the highest peaks of achievement, the climax of more than a thousand years of effort. While this was happening, however, another kind of religious song was being established in Bohemia, where the chorale—words in the Czech language and set to folk-melodies adapted for congregational use—was an important factor in the Hussite revolution.

John Huss, who learned much from the reformist writings of the English preacher John Wycliffe, denounced the extravagances of the Roman rites and the corruptness of the clergy, and taught his followers to regard the Bible as the supreme authority. Those who came after Huss allied this zeal for religious freedom with a desire also for national freedom. Many battles were fought and the elements of freedom persisted in this small country until a final defeat at the battle of the White Mountain in 1620. Throughout this period faith was nourished by the plain and popular hymnody created by the Hussites.

Wycliffe and Huss are noble figures in Western civilization because they sacrificed themselves in an endeavour to proclaim truth and to discountenance falsehood. They were driven by faith, by an inborn love of humanity, but also by reason. It was reason that gave them the power to criticize.

In the later fifteenth century many men were inspired to question long-held beliefs which had for so long been taken for granted, and to explore new avenues of thought and imagination. That this was so was partly due to an inborn zest for novelty—as we have seen the arts were never static—but more especially to the after-effects of the capture of Constantinople, the ancient Byzantine capital, by the Turks in 1453. As a result of this many Greeks escaped westward, bringing with them manuscripts relating to the culture of classical Greece, of which medieval Europe was largely unaware. Many of these manuscripts found their way to Florence, already a brilliant and lively city, and were collected into private libraries.

In the Middle Ages men had centred their thoughts on the image of God as presented by the theologians. In the new age, of the Renaissance, man himself became a focal point. Thus the term humanism is often applied. The cult of humanism therefore stimulated a greater interest in the art of living (the older traditions may sometimes appear to

Musicians at a wedding feast, fifteenth-century Florentine panel

have stressed rather more the art of dying) and hereby the arts were given a great stimulus.

We have a picture of a Florentine aristocrat of the late fifteenth century, Niccolo de' Niccoli: "when he sat at table he ate from fair antique vases, and in like manner all his table was covered with porcelain and other vessels of great beauty. . . . Some might be surprised at the many vases that he possessed, but Niccoli had friends everywhere and any who wished to give him pleasure used to send marble statues, antique vases, carvings, inscriptions, pictures done by distinguished artists, and mosaic tablets." Niccoli was so devoted to his studies that he never married, and he was also conspicuous because he had exquisite manners.

This became the model of Renaissance living. Sometimes it was outward show, masking superstition and cruelty, but sometimes it was not. In any case the attitude inspired artists of the calibre of Antonio and Piero Pollaiuolo, whose works show an understanding of the human body in movement and of landscape painting, Verrocchio, sculptor as well as painter, and Botticelli, who painted with equal skill both Christian and pagan subjects.

During the Renaissance in Italy the Church, ruled by Popes who were also inspired by the ideals of the age, absorbed much of its humanistic quality and, accordingly, gave lavish attention to artistic expression. The building of the present St. Peter's was one symbol of this; on the other hand the amount of money extracted from the further dominions of the Catholic Church was one factor in the unrest that brought about the Reformation.

The effect of the Renaissance on music may now be considered.

5

The Sixteenth Century

THE general character of the Renaissance emphasized the social, the colourful, and the scientific aspects of music, which was also enhanced by its capacity in various ways to satisfy personal vanity. There was therefore, in the sixteenth century, a great development in secular music. Above all it was the age of the madrigal.

As we have seen earlier, forms of humanism had encouraged the invention of pieces for several voices (and/or instruments), but in a period in which graceful living became an ideal not only for an Italian aristocracy but also for the middle classes in every country which looked to Italy as a cultural centre, such music became a more general luxury—if not a necessity.

At carnival time in fifteenth-century Florence songs known as *frottole*, in four parts and for men's voices, were extremely popular, and some were printed (for by now the printing of music was possible). Later *frottole* were of varied character, and sometimes for solo voice and instrumental accompaniment. These, despite often indelicate words, were designed for the more educated who in accordance with their general æsthetic interests set about refining this class of music. In this way a more acceptable poetic form was devised, which was called the madrigal— a term which had been in use in a different context a hundred years earlier.

Poems of this kind, of a lyrical quality and with occasional references to classical mythology, were given to set to the most competent composers who happened to be available. They were mostly Flemings, among whom Jacob Arcadelt, a singer at the court of the Medici family in Florence before he went to St. Peter's in Rome, and Adrian Willaert, who directed the music of St. Mark's in Venice after 1526, were the most considerable. In their madrigals Arcadelt and Willaert applied the techniques they had learned in church music, so that a similar style prevailed in both.

Madrigals were frequently composed for special social events, especially for weddings, and sometimes they were presented as dramatic pieces with the singers appropriately dressed. For a famous Florentine wedding of 1539, for instance, the madrigalists appeared in the guise of sirens, sea-monsters, sea-nymphs, shepherds, and satyrs.

The early madrigal was relatively simple in style. Soon, however, it was made into a more complex organism by such composers as Orlandus Lassus, another Fleming well known in Italy, and Andrea Gabrieli, the noted organist of St. Mark's, Venice. In their hands the parts—five was the normal number—were arranged contrapuntally, each having a distinctive melody, but within a harmonic scheme that by now was more precise and logical than formerly. The lines of melody in part-music were by now regularly supported by "common chords", and the phrase-endings fell into chordal patterns that had something of the same effect in music as marks of punctuation in literature. Moreover chords were coming to be valued for what was accepted as a particular expressive quality. The madrigals of Lassus and Gabrieli, therefore, often underline emotionally charged words with unexpected and, on that account, striking chords. There were other ways of interpreting words through music; through rhythmic alteration, the use now of high and now of low voices, and the shape of melody.

The most important composer of madrigals in the last part of the sixteenth century in Italy was Luca Marenzio. He was one of the few composers of that time who was not a church musician, even though in the service of a Roman Cardinal (who cared little about his duties as a churchman and a great deal about his secular cultural interests) and then of the Medici family in Florence. Marenzio was so famous that he was invited to Poland for a visit to the court of Sigismund III in Cracow, and he was highly favoured by many of the nobility in Italy. He published more than 200 madrigals, in which is to be found the poetry of Dante and Petrarch, as well as of his great contemporaries Tasso and Guarini, and many of these caught the attention of English travellers. So it was that a number of Marenzio's madrigals appeared in two important English collections, Nicholas Young's *Musica Transalpina* (1588) and Thomas Watson's *Italian Madrigals Englished* (*i.e.* with English translations) of 1590.

The effect of the Italian madrigal on English music was very great, just as was that of Italian poetry and romance. The age of the English madrigal was also the age of the sonnet, which was derived from Petrarch, and of Shakespeare's comedies, some of which were directly inspired by Italian models. As in the case of poets and dramatists the Elizabethan composers adopted a style and naturalized it. The English madrigal became a sensitive medium through which the most subtle points of poetic and picturesque detail could be interpreted without the music itself losing its own integrity of purpose.

The important English composers in this field were William Byrd, Thomas Morley, Thomas Weelkes, John

Wilbye, Orlando Gibbons, John Bennet, John Ward, Thomas Tomkins. But there were many others practising in many parts of the country. In general these composers, like the Italians, were employed as church musicians, but Wilbye held a post as private musician to a well-to-do middle-class family in Suffolk.

Many madrigals—like songs of all kinds and all periods —were based on love poetry, though this was often a formality, and the general impression retained after hearing a programme of such works is of the countryside. But there were no limits to the themes which the poets gave to the madrigalists. On the one hand some madrigals are akin to anthems, with solemn texts, while others—particularly those defined as *ballets*—are near to nonsense. William Byrd described a set of his own madrigals, published in 1589, as "songs of sundry natures, some of gravity and others of mirth". His introduction gives an idea of the general popularity of this form of music, when he says that his

> songs of 3, 4, 5 and 6 parts, [are] to serve for all companies and voices: whereas some are easy and plain to sing, other[s] [are] more hard and difficult, but all, such as any young practitioner in singing, with a little foresight, may easily perform.

As in Italy, so in England; the madrigal was introduced into different occasions, while the courtly function is recalled in the celebrated collection *The Triumphs of Oriana*, published two years after the death of Queen Elizabeth. This was later than was intended, for these madrigals— each ending with the phrase "Long live, fair Oriana"— were planned as a tribute to the Queen.

The madrigal was one outcome of Renaissance principles. Another was the growth of instrumental music.

King Henry VIII was an accomplished musician, and in the course of his reign he collected a vast number of instruments, all of which were carefully listed in 1547. Among the instruments were recorders of various sizes, shawms (predecessors of the oboe), also of different sizes, viols "great and small", lutes, virginals, clavichords and "portative" and "regal" organs. These instruments kept their place throughout the century, but some proved more suitable for serious musical development than others. This was particularly true of the viols, which had a soft mellow tone and which in concerted music could both support and take the place of voices. Thus we find late sixteenth-century music described as "apt for voices or viols". The viols were divided into treble, tenor, and bass; the last, being played between the legs, was called the "leg viol", or always in Italian the "viol da gamba".

The viols played as a group; so also did the recorders, and the shawms. Such groups were known as "consorts", and because they comprised instruments of one family "whole consorts". When instruments of different tone

Lute and hymn-book, from Holbein's "Ambassadors",
1533

colours were mixed, as they frequently were, then there was a "broken consort". So popular were musical instruments in the sixteenth century that numerous books were published in Germany, Italy, and Spain, describing how they should be played.

Gradually instrumental music began to establish its own reputation. In the first place transcriptions of vocal music and of dance tunes were readily available. As early as 1507, however, an Italian musician published more independent pieces for the lute, which were entitled *ricercare*. These pieces were similar to preludes or *toccatas*, and alternated between running and chordal passages. Fifty years later the ricercare settled down into a contrapuntal form, with the instrumental parts coming in, one after the other, in imitation. One composer who developed this form, and showed the way to the later *fugue*, was Adrian Willaert.

Pavans and galliards were very fashionable, and were also issued in sixteenth-century collections of lute music. Lutenists had their own form of notation, showing where the fingers were to stop the strings, called a "tablature". Lute-playing was brought to a high pitch of perfection in Spain, and to the Spanish composer Luis de Narvaez belongs the honour of being the earliest (whose music is still in existence) to write in the form of air and variations. This appears in several examples in his lute book of 1538. Another Spaniard, Miguel de Fuenllana, was a pioneer of solo song with lute accompaniment.

Under the Emperor Charles V Spain became a great power, commanding the seas and colonizing the new world of Mexico and Peru, and defeating the French in the battle for control of Italy. Power and confidence were given expression through music, and wealth afforded the opportunity for its cultivation and enjoyment.

The most notable composer of instrumental music in Spain in the first half of the sixteenth century was Antonio de Cabezón, who, like the earlier Florentine Landino, was blind. Cabezón was an organist and clavichord player, and he was in the service of Charles V's queen, the Empress Isobel. After her death he was made a member of the household of Prince Philip, later Philip II, under whom the Armada set out on its ill-fated expedition

Maiolica inkstand in the form of a boy playing on the organ. Made at Urbino, c. 1565

against England in 1588. As a member of the royal household Cabezón travelled widely in the Empire—to Italy, the Netherlands, and Germany, and in 1554 he had been in the retinue which accompanied Philip to England on the occasion of his marriage with Queen Mary.

Cabezón was a great organist, and, understanding the special qualities of the instrument, he composed for it in a striking and individual manner. His variations, or "verses", which he composed to be played between the sung verses of plainsong hymns, sowed the seeds of the characteristic organ work of later times, the "chorale prelude". Cabezón also composed for harp and the Spanish *vihuela*, or guitar, sometimes basing variations on folk-melodies.

Among the instruments belonging to Henry VIII we noticed the virginals. This instrument, so popular in England, stimulated what is perhaps the most rewarding keyboard music of the whole period: music that is not only enchanting to hear, but also to play.

The virginals (usually spelt thus in the plural) was a simpler version of the harpsichord, a small oblong box which could be placed on a table. Like the harpsichord the strings of the virginals (one to each key as opposed to the two of the harpsichord) were plucked. This mode of producing sound was taken over from the medieval psaltery, whereas the striking action of the clavichord and piano derives from the ancient dulcimer. The virginals was regarded as a suitable instrument for a lady, and Queen Elizabeth, as also her cousin Mary of Scotland, was an excellent player. This being the case, and she not being averse from its being known, there was every encouragement to English composers to favour the instrument.

There was, indeed, a flood of virginals music: the most famous, but by no means the only, manuscript collection being the *Fitzwilliam Virginal Book*. Among the composers of virginals music were William Byrd, Thomas Morley, and Orlando Gibbons, already noted as leading madrigalists, John Bull, famous for his executant skill also in the cities of northern Europe, Giles Farnaby, a Cornishman with a whimsical imagination, and Martin Peerson.

As in all early instrumental music there was in the virginals repertoire a large amount of rearranged vocal music, some sacred but also much that was secular. Folk-

tunes and contemporary ballads served as the basis for
variations that were often brilliant. There were dances,
pavans, galliards, and almans, as well as rougher measures
from, say, Ireland or Wales, and set dances from the court
masques and entertainments. Fantasias, or fancies, and
toccatas were independently instrumental in character.

Lady at the virginals, from an engraving by Goltzius, c. 1600

On occasion composers also tried their skill in "programme music", that is music which attempts to be descriptive and narrative. Among such music were Byrd's "The Bells" and even more famous "Battle". This is a suite of pieces, each section clearly showing the style of the content: "The March before the Battle; The Soldier's Summons—the March of Footmen; The March of Horsemen; Now follow with the trumpets; The Irish March; the Bagpipe; And the drone; The flute and the drum; The March to the Fight; The Retreat. Now followeth a galliard for the victory."

The picture of Renaissance music so far shows the development of the secular madrigal as a recreation in town and country house, a general love of instrumental music and a particular advance in keyboard music and technique. To this should be added a deeper scientific interest in the theory and practice of the art, resulting in the publication of important works by the Swiss writer Glareanus, who added the present major and minor scales to the "modes" which had been allowed by the medieval scholars to church music, and the Venetian Zarlino, whose theories led in the direction of "classical" harmony and even of the system of tuning known as equal temperament. Such books were freely discussed not only by professional musicians but also by cultivated amateurs, who were by the end of the sixteenth century able to possess considerable libraries of music, some printed but much in manuscript volumes.

As has been suggested the general cultivation of music owed much to the enthusiastic example of the leaders of society—kings, princes, dukes, and worldly princes of the Church.

Music, from the humanists' point of view, added grace and colour to life, and it also animated the sister arts. As yet there was no opera, but large-scale shows and pageants, especially at the courts of Italy, France and England, were preparing a way for it.

In 1571 two Frenchmen, the poet Antoine de Baïf and the musician Thibault de Courville, founded an "Academy" (such societies devoted to all branches of knowledge were a feature of the Renaissance) for the joint study of music and poetry, and its deliberations influenced many artists at court. In 1581 these artists were given a great opportunity when commanded by Henry III to prepare a great display in honour of the marriage of the Queen's sister to the Duke of Joyeux. The outcome was *Circe*, a ballet.

No expense was spared to make this work a great success, less for the sake of the bridal pair than for the glory of France. It would symbolize for visiting ambassadors the wealth and power of the country—particularly important in view of the recent disruption caused by wars of religion. *Circe* was artistically significant because it had what other similar entertainments had not, a consistent plot.

The music for *Circe* was superintended by Claude le Jeune, one of the most renowned musicians in Paris. Le Jeune was important in other fields. He was a Huguenot, and had set a number of the Huguenot psalm-tunes in motet style. In 1588 he was arrested during the siege of Paris on account of his religious beliefs, and a Catholic soldier was about to burn his precious manuscripts: fortunately, however, a Catholic musician, a friend of Le Jeune, managed to persuade the soldier not to carry out his intention, and the manuscripts were saved. That is not the only time in history when music has served to unite men of opposed beliefs.

Secular music directly reflected the humanistic aspect of the Renaissance, and, despite the necessary technical connection between it and sacred music, therefore may be taken to be of prime importance. The secular musicians were busy in establishing the right of music to be an art independent of religious control as well as their own rights in society.

At the same time church music was of tremendous significance. In it is seen the culmination of centuries of skill and effort in choral music, and at least half a dozen composers, whose special province was church music, must be ranked among the immortal composers of all time.

We return to Rome, where the new St. Peter's, richly coloured under Julius II and the splendour-loving Medici Pope Leo X by the genius of Michelangelo and Raphael, attracted so many musicians. They were members of the two choirs, the Julian, founded in 1513 by Julius II, and the Sistine, which was the Pope's own choir belonging to the Sistine Chapel. As has been seen, Frenchmen and Flemings were at first given pride of place, but by the middle of the sixteenth century Italian musicians succeeded to positions of eminence. Among them were Giovanni Animuccia, director of the Julian Choir, and Giovanni Pierluigi da Palestrina, who was associated with both choirs and also other churches in Rome. Animuccia and Palestrina were also friendly with the unconventional priest Philip Neri (now St. Philip), who instituted an association between music and religion that was later to grow into the *oratorio*.

Roman church music of the sixteenth century represents a peak in the development of music, for the composers, particularly Palestrina, their leader, blended the intellectual skill of Flemish music, and sometimes its passion and colour, with an Italian fluency. The masses and motets of Palestrina, in which the parts interweave with marvellous individuality yet within the clear harmonic principles of the age, are classical in balance, pro-

St. Peter's, Rome

portion, and economy. Palestrina sometimes coloured his
music, as the madrigalists, with musical representation of
the more pictorial words, but he never allowed this to
detract from the consistent, logical flow of the music.
More importantly, he did not permit his music to impede
the movement of the liturgy. Among Palestrina's most
notable works are the twelve-part setting of the medieval
poem *Stabat Mater* ("The Mother was standing by the
Cross") and the Mass dedicated to Pope Marcellus II
and therefore known as the *Missa Papæ Marcelli*. It should,
however, be realized that the music of Palestrina sounded

less austere in the sixteenth century, for the singers lavishly decorated the notes set before them. This is no longer done, because the art of decoration was an extempore art and its tradition was lost.

Palestrina and the other church musicians of Rome were made aware of a new and more strict attitude to liturgical music. Because powerful members of the Church of Rome were alive to the abuses that sparked off the Reformation in other countries, a great Council, the Council of Trent, was called to reconsider the affairs of the Church and its liturgy with the intention of rooting out all abuses. The Council met between 1545 and 1563. So far as music was concerned, it was laid down that it should be free of "impure elements", "secular forms", and "unedifying language". The works of Palestrina were held in high favour because it was felt that in them was the nearest approach to a model style. This opinion has been expressed by successive Popes in official documents, and many others have also subscribed to it.

The music of the Sistine Chapel was traditionally unaccompanied, and so it has remained to the present day. It is often thought that all Catholic church music of the sixteenth century was unaccompanied, but this was by no means the case.

In St. Mark's, Venice, indeed, the splendour of the music was greatly enhanced by the rich quality of the brass and stringed instruments that were employed. Great Venetian composers of that age were Claudio Merulo, an organist who was one of the pioneers of the toccata, and Giovanni Gabrieli.

The same general style of composition in church music was common to all parts of Europe, but there were regional characteristics. Venetian music differed from that of Rome. Spanish music, although written by composers with intimate experience of Italy, gave the effect of great devotion; this was especially true of the intense works of Victoria and Morales. English music, represented by Tallis and Byrd, was often harder, and marked by a much freer use of discord.

In England the Reformation did not alter substantially the pattern of worship, and the Church of England gave many opportunities to its musicians, who now composed anthems rather than motets, services rather than masses, in which the same musical principles remained constant.

The music of the sixteenth century which has been considered so far is contrapuntal, with the separate voices frequently imitating each other as in earlier canon and later fugue. Contrast is obtained, however, by chordal passages, which have great dignity because based on the fundamental major and minor chords. Rhythm is relatively free because the music was not bound to metrical patterns (as must necessarily be the case in, for example, dance music), nor to bar-lines (which were not written in the parts from which singers sang at that time).

However Palestrina and other masters tried to simplify church music they could only succeed up to a point; for contrapuntal music is by its nature complicated and intellectual. The radical simplification of sacred music was brought about by factors that lay outside the field of music itself. Two monuments to the sixteenth century are the French psalm-tune and the German chorale. Both are owed to the determination of Reformers that the laity should have their rights, as well as their responsibilities, assured within new organizations.

The French psalm-tune is owed to the followers of John Calvin, the French theologian, who made his headquarters in Geneva in 1536. Among those who accepted Calvin's teaching were the poets Clément Marot and

John Calvin

Théodore Béza, who wrote metrical versions of the Psalms. When Marot produced his translations in this form he was forced to flee from France to Geneva, and then to Italy, where he died in 1544. At the same time, Thomas Sternhold, an official at the court of Henry VIII, was busy making similar English versions of the Psalms. The Calvinistic devotion to the Psalter arose from a conviction, not shared by the Lutherans, that only what appeared in the Bible should be admitted to the realm of church music. This conviction had also been held by the earliest Fathers of the Christian Church.

It was fortunate for Calvinism, and for Protestant church music generally, that the arrangement and composition of suitable music was at an early date in the hands of Louis Bourgeois. Bourgeois took melodies from German sources (for Calvin had spent some time in Strasbourg), from French sacred and secular songs, and from earlier hymns of the church, adapted them to the metres of Marot and Béza, and harmonized them with great simplicity.

96

The final form of the *Genevan Psalter* was issued in 1562, and contained the work of other men, conspicuous among whom was Claude Goudimel. Goudimel, distinguished as a composer of Catholic church music in earlier life, was murdered in Lyons in 1572, during the Massacre of St. Bartholomew.

The Psalms and their music affected English and Scottish worship and music in that many Psalters, containing melodies from Geneva, were published in the latter half of the sixteenth century—and afterwards. Some parts of Germany, where Calvinism made converts, also adopted music from Genevan sources; so too did the Swiss Protestants who had been taught by Ulrich Zwingli, who was killed in the religious wars of his country in 1531.

Many melodies from Geneva and from the English Psalters which were based on the Genevan are to be found in all hymn-books in current use, not only in the Protestant Churches of Europe but also of America and the British Commonwealth.

Music of this order may be described as utilitarian, designed for a purpose and suitable for no other. It is self-contained and, unlike liturgical music of the Catholic traditions, not to be "enjoyed"—even though it may be admired—as music in its own right. In this also is its strength.

Lutheran music, on the other hand, is more attractive and more varied. From the popular chorale, indeed, has sprung some of the noblest music ever conceived.

Martin Luther, the one-time Augustinian monk, was a trained musician and a great lover of the hymns, sequences, and antiphons of the old Church. He lived in a country where the transition from Latin hymnody to the language of the people had already begun. In the later Middle Ages many hymns had been translated from Latin,

Martin Luther

and many others had been originally composed in German. Bohemian song-books, the work of the Hussites, were published in Germany at the beginning of the sixteenth century, and these had a great influence in Saxony, Luther's native country, stimulating the production of a Lutheran collection of sacred music. The first Lutheran hymns, twenty-one out of thirty-seven of which were written by Luther himself, were published in 1523. Also engaged in the composition of hymns for the German people was Hans Sachs—the hero of Wagner's *Mastersingers*, who was at one time forbidden by the town council of Nürnberg to publish such works. An early collaborator on the musical side was Johann Walther, chief musician—or *Kapellmeister* —to the Elector of Saxony.

The music of the Lutheran hymn, like that of the Genevan psalm, came from various sources. Composers of eminence to arrange the music were Hans Leo Hassler, Michael Prætorius and Johann Crüger. Hassler was one of a number of German composers who had studied in

Venice with Giovanni Gabrieli, and he composed much Latin church music as well as madrigals. Michael Præ-torius was a leading theoretical writer, as well as a com-poser, and his authoritative accounts of the techniques of sixteenth- and seventeenth-century organ building have exercised a considerable influence on modern organ design. Crüger worked in Berlin, and his magnificent settings are evidence of the wealth of music that was not only permitted but welcomed by the music-loving German Lutherans. To such men Johann Sebastian Bach was much indebted, for their chorale melodies (as well as those of many other composers) served as the foundation of most of his output for the Lutheran church of the eighteenth century.

Many of the chorales associated with Bach are to be found in his settings of the story of the *Passion*. One of the features of Lutheran church life, taken over from the prac-tice of the pre-Reformation church, was a form of musical setting of the *Passion*. Johann Walther, Luther's friend, was the first composer of a Lutheran *Passion*, in which the main characters of the drama chanted in plainsong while the words of the crowd were given to a four-part choir. Walther's *Passion* was composed about the year 1523, and it was performed with great regularity, especially in Leip-zig, for many years. The last recorded performance was in 1806. This form of *Passion* was related to religious drama, for the division of parts among solo voices clearly indicated a feeling for vocal characterization at least.

Another way of setting the Passion story was in the motet style, always with the text allotted to two or more voices arranged contrapuntally. Among the composers of Motet-Passions were Johannes Galliculus, the first German composer of such a work, Jakob Handl, a fine Bohemian musician, and Joachim von Burgk, whose St. John Passion was the first to a text in German.

In all this early Passion music is seen the union of the old and the new. The spirit of the Renaissance shows in a greater feeling for dramatic expression, for a more humanistic interpretation, and in the conception of music as the heritage of the common people—the congregation.

In Protestant church music of the sixteenth century we become aware of a democratic stirring in the art and a broader significance for the techniques of composing skill that had hitherto been zealously guarded, and controlled so far as was possible, by the pre-Reformation Catholic Church.

The importance of congregational music, in the sixteenth century, is summarized in the Introduction to the fine hymn-book (*Gesangbuch*) of the Swiss Evangelical Reformed Church of the present day:

> In song the congregation answers to the Word of God. It is born from the Word of God. In it the Church recognizes its Faith; through it the Church seeks God's help and thanks Him for His goodness; it is the means whereby we praise God's grace and majesty. In hard times it is both strength and comfort, and in good days our joy.

6

Age of Experiment

THE institution of new religious creeds and the growth of new church organizations in the sixteenth century was caused partly by a general dissatisfaction with abuse and corruption, partly by a broadening of educational opportunity, and partly by strong national and regional traditions and outlooks. In the various forms of church music which began to flourish as a result of the Reformation national characteristics were at least more noticeable than formerly: thus we may speak of the particular English quality of the anthems of the Church of England, and the German quality of Lutheran chorales and Passions —even though the basic style in both cases, as also in the psalm-tune as harmonized by the French, derived from the "universal" idiom of pre-Reformation church music.

The style in which Catholic church music was composed was still, in a sense, universal as the sixteenth turned into the seventeenth century. After all, apart from masses and motets, madrigals were in high favour, and in them the contrapuntal ordering of part-singing was as near perfection as could be.

But in the early part of the seventeenth century the style itself collapsed. The revolution which brought about this collapse can be summed up as simply as this: melody became an end in itself. The reformers of church music, in all creeds, were agreed on one point—that music should be made more simple. Simplicity became a word freely used by musicians and also by those lovers of music who were its chief patrons on the secular side.

We need to look again at one special side of the meaning of Renaissance; that which led back to classical Greece. Nowhere was this more discussed than in Florence, and in Florence none were keener in speculation on classical topics than those who frequented the palace of Giovanni Bardi.

Bardi, Count of Vernio, was a characteristic Florentine figure. He was of noble birth and by virtue of his rank became chamberlain to Pope Clement VIII. He was a scholar and a mathematician, belonging to some of the learned societies for which Renaissance Florence was famous. He was a writer in a modest way, possibly even a composer. Most of all he was a delightful and stimulating host, and in late middle age enjoyed the company of the most forward-looking of the musicians of the city.

Entertainments with music were commonplace at every European court, but on the whole they were too loose in structure, too uncertain in dramatic intention, and too casual in regard to music, to appear as satisfactory works of art to keen and logical minds. The current madrigal style when applied dramatically led to absurdity—with four or five singers trying rather ineffectually to do the work of one.

The rule of economy is a good one to apply to art, and so it proved in this case. One of Bardi's friends was Vincenzo Galilei, father of the astronomer, and he declaimed against the complexities of contemporary part-writing in an essay on "ancient and modern music". This he followed with settings of an episode from the fourteenth canto of Dante's *Purgatory*, and a passage from the

Lamentations of Jeremiah, for solo voices with accompaniment. These settings met with an encouraging reception. Next came a more ambitious scheme. The fable of *Dafne*, as told by the poet Ottavia Rinuccini, was made into a consistent musico-dramatic piece—still with solo voices supported by slender accompaniment. This, by now called the *Stilo Rappresentativo* (the "representative style"), was also acclaimed. The Grand Duke of Tuscany, Cosimo di Medici, was impressed, not least perhaps by reason of the fact that his director of music, Jacopo Peri, had collaborated with Giulio Caccini and Jacopo Corsi in supplying the music; and he commanded a setting of Rinuccini's *Euridice* to celebrate the wedding of Maria di Medici with Henry IV of France.

Euridice was performed, Peri himself singing the part of Orpheus, for the first time at the Palazzo Pitti in Florence on October 6, 1600. The score of this work, the first real opera, was published during the next year. Another setting of *Euridice* was made by Caccini, who appears to have been somewhat jealous of Peri's success. Perhaps he had some reason, for it was Caccini who made the first experiments in *recitative* (in supposed imitation of the Greek manner of singing) for the benefit of Count Bardi. Caccini was otherwise important because of *Le nuove musiche* (1602) in which he published *airs*, as well as madrigals, and a Preface which described the art of singing. The importance of melody is thus underlined. The accompaniment of vocal melody was set down by Caccini as a single bass line with which there were figures indicating the chords the accompanist should play. This sort of bass was known as "figured bass" or as "basso continuo", and the principle thus established remained in use for almost two hundred years.

The aim of these pioneers of opera was expression of a

dramatic idea through the medium of music, with the reservation that the music should not impede the drama. Musical expression depends on variety and contrast; drama can be illuminated at certain points by music which is realistic: these were points for the future and after Peri's and Caccini's experimental work opera awaited the touch of genius. This came from one of the splendidly exciting characters in musical history—Claudio Monteverdi, sometime musician to the Duke of Mantua before succeeding to the directorship of the music in St. Mark's, Venice, in 1613. There Monteverdi enjoyed great prestige and a brilliant team of thirty singers and twenty-five instrumentalists.

When the Duke of Mantua noticed the success attaching to Florentine opera he asked Monteverdi to produce such a work for him. The result was *Orfeo*, which far surpassed anything previously achieved. Monteverdi, in the prime of life, had hitherto composed church music and, especially, madrigals which were characterized by a profound emotional quality often marked by daring changes of tonality. Monteverdi transferred this emotional quality to opera in which he made a clear distinction between recitative and aria, and in so doing brought the story vividly to life. There was also the orchestra, of which the possibilities were ignored by Peri and Caccini. For *Orfeo* Monteverdi used this extensive body of players:

2 *gravicembali* (harpsichords), 2 *violini piccoli alla Francese* (violins of the kind favoured in France), 10 *viole de brazzo* (treble and tenor viols), 3 *bassi da gamba* (bass viols), 2 *contrabassi da viola* (double basses), 1 *flautino* (small flute or recorder), 2 *cornetti* ("cornets"—*i.e.* high-pitched wind instruments made of wood or ivory and covered with leather), 1 *clarino* (trumpet with a small horn on which high notes could be played with ease), 3 *trombe sordini*

(trumpets with mutes), 4 *tromboni*, 1 *regalo* (portable organ), and 2 *chitarroni* (bass lutes).

Monteverdi's orchestration—he used the tone qualities of instruments and groups of instruments in an individual manner—his understanding of the human voice, his deep appreciation of dramatic climax, and his sense of musical form and architecture, lifted opera to a quite different plane.

After *Orfeo* Monteverdi wrote *Arianne*, also for the theatre in Mantua. The Venetians had no intention of being left out in the cold, and in 1624 Monteverdi composed his *Il combattimento di Tancredi e Clorinda* at the instigation of a Venetian senator; this, with many sound effects—such as *tremolo* and *pizzicato*—used for the first time, was another landmark in the history of opera. Many of Monteverdi's operas were lost in the sack of Mantua in 1631, but two of his latest works, *Il ritorno d'Ulisse in patria* (1641) and *L'incorronazione di Poppea* (1642) show the pattern of opera that was to prevail in the eighteenth century. The singers, now trained to make the best use of their voices in *bel canto*, were given dramatic recitatives, and long arias requiring great skill and powers of expression in the *da capo* form (that is—A, B, A), while the orchestra consisted basically of the string ensemble and harpsichord.

The vogue for opera meant the building of new opera houses, in Bologna, in Rome (where the opera house of 1632 could accommodate an audience of 3,000), and in Venice, where the first public opera house (of San Cassiano) in the world was opened in 1637. There were, of course, other composers of opera, though none of the status of Monteverdi. Among them were Michele Angelo Rossi and Luigi Rossi, who were patronized by the Barberini family of Rome. Luigi was invited to Paris by Cardinal Mazarin, a friend of the Barberinis, and his opera *Orfeo* (the subject has been much favoured since the earliest days of opera) was produced there in 1647. The opera was a success, but its production gave an opportunity to those who disliked Cardinal Mazarin's politics to attack him; accordingly the Cardinal decided not to embark again on such ventures.

Thirteen years later, however, another Italian composer —Pietro Cavalli, pupil of Monteverdi and *maestro di capella* of St. Mark's, Venice—was invited to Paris to produce an opera. This was for the marriage of Louis XIV to Maria Theresa, and was performed in the Grand Gallery of the Palace of the Louvre. The opera was *Xerse*, composed for Venice some eight years earlier. To the original score Louis XIV's favourite composer, Lully, made additions. Cavalli visited Paris twice, and was also once in Innsbruck in Austria, where another opera graced another royal occasion. In all Cavalli wrote 42 operas.

In the seventeenth century Italian song (for opera was dominated by its singers) conquered Europe for the second time; the first had been when the missionaries had planted plainsong in strange lands. In France opera developed

St. Mark's, Venice

under the brilliant direction of Jean Baptiste Lully, who, however, adapted it to French taste and his own talents. The operas of Lully were different from those of the Italians (Lully although Italian-born was a naturalized Frenchman) in that he used French texts, employed a simpler kind of aria akin to the native *chanson*, introduced ballet music, and prefaced them with overtures in the French style. These overtures were to be the model for Handel in the eighteenth century.

Italian musicians went to Germany. One of them was Carlo Pallavicini, a Venetian, who became Kapellmeister to the Elector of Saxony in Dresden, where he directed the new opera. At an early date there were opera houses in Leipzig and Hamburg, and by the beginning of the eighteenth century there was not a town of any consequence in Germany without its opera.

In England on the other hand the "new style" made much less impact, even though many travellers—including the diarist John Evelyn—were enchanted by what they saw and heard in Italy. In the early part of the seventeenth century madrigal composition went on apace. The style, however, became generally simpler, and the melody of the highest voice more dominant. At the same time solo song with lute accompaniment was brought to a high degree of perfection by such composers as the poet-musician Thomas Campion, William Rosseter, and John Dowland. The last, sometime lutenist at the Danish court, was one of the great masters of solo song.

Another notable composer of this school was Alphonso Ferrabosco, son of an Italian musician who had come to the court of Queen Elizabeth. Ferrabosco composed airs (or "ayres") which were designed for the masques which graced the Palace of Whitehall during the reign of James I. These masques, of which the texts were most often by Ben

Jonson and the designs by Inigo Jones, continued a familiar pattern of court entertainment. Those responsible for them in Jacobean and Caroline times prepared sumptuous and beautiful shows, in which the poetry is often of the highest beauty, and their patrons were well contented. Nicholas Lanier, in 1617, did proudly introduce a brief display of *stilo recitativo*, but no one took the hint and turned to Italian-style opera.

Political disturbances, civil war, the period of the Commonwealth, gave people other things to consider than artistic theories. So far as opera was concerned the English missed the boat. They have continued to miss this particular boat ever since.

The Restoration of the Monarchy in the person of Charles II revived the spirits of artists, but drama, so well served for so long, and literature took precedence over music. Charles enjoyed music and encouraged his musicians to take note of developments in France such as he had witnessed during his exile. The royal band of violins was constituted on the pattern of that at Versailles, and opera of a sort was staged in the theatre. English opera, however, comprised incidental songs and instrumental pieces for spoken plays. The music was introduced as no more than a diversion. Into this situation, however, stepped one genius: Henry Purcell.

Purcell, court musician and organist of Westminster Abbey, was consistently employed as a theatre composer from the age of twenty-one, and there remains a large body of his songs originally written for plays by Durfey, Davenant, Dryden, Shadwell, Congreve, and for various adaptations of plays by Shakespeare. Among the larger entertainments were Dryden's *King Arthur*, the curious transformation of *A Midsummer Night's Dream* into *The Fairy Queen*, and *The Tempest*. In these works are fine choruses, dances, and incidental pieces which display a vivid dramatic sensibility and sometimes a striking capacity to render humour—as in the "drunken poet" scene of the *Fairy Queen*—in terms of music.

The climax of Purcell's operatic career, however, lies in *Dido and Aeneas*. In this tiny masterpiece, written for a girls' school in Chelsea, Purcell blends the styles of Italian recitative (enriched by his own dynamic melodic gift and his feeling for verbal meaning and accentuation), French choral and string writing, with the melodic idiom of English folk-music, and the athletic tradition of the older masque.

This was the beginning of English opera. It was, as will be seen, also almost the end.

All vocal music of the seventeenth century may be discovered to demand a high technique. The term *bel canto* has already been introduced. It means, literally, "beautiful singing", and was the aim of every singing-teacher, of which there were many, in Italy at that time. Not only did singers perform in opera, but also privately at the musical parties which were a feature of polite living. For such occasions Italian singers were furnished with cantatas. A cantata was a work in several movements, of recitatives and arias, based on a polite sequence of verses which made a more or less consistent story. Such cantatas began to appear about 1620, and among the early composers of cantatas were Marc' Antonio Cesti—yet another member of the Venetian school of opera composers—and Alessandro Stradella.

The serious-minded Germans turned their attention to a religious variant of the form, and Franz Tunder, of Lübeck, composed cantatas based on chorale melodies, thus taking German music one step nearer the art of Bach.

Whether secular or sacred, the solo cantata, the voice

supported only by harpsichord and string bass, gave opportunity for vocal display and for the concentration of the listener on the melodic line, now smooth and flowing, now broken into brilliant divisions or runs, now adorned with shakes or other graces, but always passionate and expressive.

What the voice could do the stringed instrument could also do. Stringed instruments were melodic in character, subtle and expressive; and of all this family the most attractive was the violin. Out of favour went the less flexible and coarser-voiced wind instruments, and, gradually, the old family of viols. The viols lived on in England rather longer than in most other countries, and fine chamber music in the form of *Fancies* or *Fantasias* were written for private pleasure until this form came to a climax in the nine masterly Fantasias in four parts of Henry Purcell.

Violin makers were busy in Brescia and Cremona, in London, and in Innsbruck. Italian players rapidly developed a compelling technique, including double and triple stopping, and taught the art to other nations. Above all the Germans were quick learners.

Singers had *cantatas* (pieces for singing), instrumentalists *sonatas* (pieces to be "sounded", *i.e.* played). Sonatas for one or two violins, harpsichord (the part played, or "realized", from a figured bass), and 'cello (or gamba), were written by Giovanni Vitali, Giovanni Bassani, Arcangelo Corelli, and Henry Purcell—who claimed in this field to be following the best Italian examples. Sonatas were works generally of four movements, and they gradually took on a character independent of the suites and canzonas from which they derived.

The most spectacular advances in instrumental music, however, were with the keyboard instruments. Great virtuoso players of the organ, performing in churches and cathedrals, and educating and delighting vast numbers of people for whom music of the highest quality was only here available, flourished in Italy, Germany and the Netherlands, where the finest organs were built.

Living in Amsterdam as organist of the church in which the great painter Rembrandt was christened was Jan Sweelinck, who had been a pupil of Andrea Gabrieli in Venice. Sweelinck joined two ages: his motets and psalms are of the sixteenth-century tradition, but his fugues for organ were pioneer works in the form brought to its peak by Bach. The link between Sweelinck and Bach was direct, for among those who journeyed to Amsterdam to hear him play was Samuel Scheidt, who became organist in the Moritzkirche in Handel's birthplace—Halle, in Saxony. Scheidt treated chorale melodies as organ pieces, turning them into variations, or chorale preludes; an art further developed by another great German organist, Johann Pachelbel of Nürnberg.

The greatest of seventeenth-century Italian organists was Girolamo Frescobaldi, organist of St. Peter's, Rome. Frescobaldi, who was also a composer of madrigals, wrote fugue-like pieces entitled *ricercari* and *canzone*, but also brilliant *toccatas*. One of his pupils was Johann Froberger, who became court organist in Vienna, and Froberger wrote works in similar style to his master and so helped to establish the Italian manner in Germany. Thus the organ proceeded towards its latter-day eminence as a peculiarly "religious" instrument, largely devoted to forms of music that were inspired by various liturgies, but principally the Lutheran.

The general maid-of-all-work among keyboard instruments, both in the seventeenth and eighteenth centuries, was the harpsichord, which with its clear, acid tone-quality and its percussive edge enjoys a remarkable revival at the present time. The best makers of harpsichords were in the Netherlands, and the most celebrated name is that of the family Ruckers, of Antwerp. The influence of the Ruckers manufactory was considerable, extending throughout Germany and France and, after the middle of the seventeenth century when the instrument largely replaced the smaller virginals and spinets, England.

Large harpsichords resembled the organ in possessing more than one manual, or keyboard. Another similarity lay in the provision of stops, by which the harpsichordist was able to employ 4 feet, 8 feet, or 16 feet tones, and even (through using the "lute" stop) to make the instrument alter its character. There any resemblance to the organ ends. The harpsichord is frequently described as a predecessor of the pianoforte. In a way it is, but, because of the great difference in tonal quality and character, it is important not to think of harpsichord music as equally satisfactory on the piano. The smoother tone of the piano obscures the details, especially of ornamentation, which belong exclusively to the harpsichord. With the great development of instrumental music in the seventeenth century we begin to notice that the character of a particular instrument determines in part the nature of the music composed for it.

As we have seen (on p. 104) the harpsichord had its place in the orchestral ensemble. Here it blended with voices and other instruments and was invaluable for building harmonies from the "figured bass", especially in recitatives and arias. It was a French musician, Jacques Champion de Chambonnières, who first realized the immense independent possibilities of the harpsichord. He was harpsichordist both to Louis XIII and Louis XIV, but also court musician for a time in Sweden and Brandenburg. He

Harpsichord, 1766

was a fine player, and like all early virtuoso performers found it necessary to make his own repertoire. Much of his music for harpsichord resembled that which belonged to the ubiquitous lute. His dances, which he arranged into suites, were those which were already popular—particularly sarabandes and pavanes. But Chambonnières spaced his chords more aptly for the keyboard and, above all, added the charm of ornamentation that reflects the exquisite taste of the furnishings and embellishments of Versailles.

Chambonnières published *Pièces de clavessin* (*claveçin*, or harpsichord) in 1670, and prepared the items with instructions on how to play the ornaments.

Chambonnières was a great figure at the French court, and through his influence the Couperin family were there employed. The most famous of the Couperins was François, the second of his name, known as "le Grand". François Couperin, whose harpsichord pieces are among the most charming ever written for this instrument, called his suites *Ordres*, and to the individual items he frequently gave descriptive titles. Titles such as *L'Arlequine, Les*

A lesson on the harpsichord

Charmes, *La Lugubre*, *La Pantomime*, suggest ideas which lie outside music. We expect the music to be picturesque, even narrative; we are not disappointed. Programme music— a term particularly applied to music of the nineteenth century—was by no means unknown in the seventeenth and eighteenth centuries. At the very end of the seventeenth century the German composer Johann Kuhnau, predecessor of Bach at the School of St. Thomas in Leipzig, issued a set of *Biblical Sonatas*, which were intended to illustrate episodes in the Old Testament. One of the most popular of these was the sonata which depicted the defeat of Goliath by David.

The development of instrumental music depended on private interest and leisure. Opera and church music were public exhibitions, and circumscribed by external considerations of plot on the one hand and liturgy on the other. There being no public concerts or recitals, all other fields of music were subject to the whims, enthusiasm, and purse of the aristocratic or royal patron. It is to him that we owe the form of the suite, the sonata, the cantata, and the concerto.

Concerto, like many other terms which have come to have a particular meaning, was applied at the beginning of the seventeenth century to almost any piece of "concerted" music. By the end of the century concerto was applied properly to music, structurally similar to the four-movement sonata, for a group of string players (supported by one or two harpsichords). This group was divided into two sections, one small and the other rather larger. The small section, often comprising the two violins and 'cello of the popular instrumental sonata, was known as the *concertino* (little concerto); the larger, contrasting, section as the *concerto grosso* (large concerto). This disposition gave fullness and contrast of tone, and also the opportunity to the composer to construct movements of greater length.

Composers who were pioneers in concerto were the Italians Giuseppe Torelli, of Bologna, where he directed the orchestra of a church before going to the German court of the Margrave of Brandenburg, Alessandro Stradella, and Arcangelo Corelli. The last was blessed with an indulgent patron, the Cardinal Ottoboni, who took great pride in the accomplishments of his musicians. On each Monday evening the Cardinal gave a concert at his palace in Rome, to which came every distinguished visitor to Rome. Corelli had a brilliant understanding of string technique and of the possibilities of the string ensemble. He put his opportunities to good purpose, and his sonatas and *concerti grossi* became models for all composers in these forms for many years. Among those who benefited from introduction to Corelli, at the beginning of the eighteenth century, was a young composer from Saxony—George Frideric Händel, in whose own *concerti grossi* the influence of Corelli may be felt.

The seventeenth century was, in a sense, a period of experiment in music. In painting, on the other hand, it was an age of fulfilment, especially in Holland. It was the era of Rembrandt and Rubens, of Hals, Vermeer, de Hooch, and many others. Anyone who has looked at half a dozen works by these masters will almost certainly have come across a family group—a middle-class family—engaged in some sort of musical activity. This symbolizes the great spread of musical interest, and gives promise of a new force in the cultivation of music and musicians.

The record of England, despite the genius of Purcell, seems somewhat pale beside the more colourful accounts of musical performance in the courts of Europe. If, however, reference is made to the Diary of Samuel Pepys it will be discovered that in England at that time there was a considerable zest for the art, and that this was not limited to the most influential members of the community.

Pepys took lessons in singing and in theorbo-playing (the theorbo was a bass lute, and it continued in use in England until the mid-eighteenth century, when it was used by Handel). He played the flageolet and the flute—usually after his supper; the viol and the violin—the latter sometimes as a cure for melancholy. He was a composer in a modest way, and had somewhat intolerant opinions concerning other people's music and performance. The self-portrait drawn by Pepys is engaging and also instructive, for it shows the social value of music. Pepys gives one moving illustration of the middle-class love of music. When the great fire of 1666 broke out the citizens of London took to the river as quickly as possible. They took with them the few precious belongings that they could carry:

"River full of lighters," wrote Pepys on September 2, 1666, "and boats taking in goods, and good goods swimming in the water, and only I observed that hardly one lighter or boat in three that had the goods of a house in, but there was a pair of Virginalls in it."

Among Pepys's acquaintances was one John Banister. Banister's talent as violinist had been brought to the notice of Charles II, by whom he was sent to France to perfect his skill. In due course Banister was appointed leader of the King's band of violins, only to lose his place when he criticized the King for bringing in a French musician to superintend some part of the royal music. Banister then devoted himself to free-lance work, to teaching, to arranging music for the theatre, and to writing. In 1672 he had a brainwave, which resulted in the following newspaper advertisement:

These are to give notice that at Mr. John Banister's

house, now called the Musick-School, over against the George Tavern in White Friars, this present Monday, will be musick performed by excellent masters, beginning precisely at four of the clock in the afternoon, and every afternoon for the future, precisely at the same hour.

John Banister continued his concerts until his death six years later. Others followed his example, and in the last quarter of the seventeenth century many public concerts were given. Sometimes these took place in taverns, in the large rooms of dancing academies, and at the "consort-room" in York Buildings, Villiers Street, near Charing Cross. Here Purcell's *Ode for St. Cecilia's Day* was sung in 1693. Music by John Blow was also performed. Singers and players from abroad joined with native artists, and occasionally the concerts were attended by visiting royalty. The concert-room in Villiers Street was in use for many years, and in 1732 this was where Handel's first oratorio *Esther* (though this was not its first performance) was sung.

This democratization of music bore rich fruit, for it made possible the conditions which stimulated Handel to compose the works by which he is now best known—his oratorios.

At this point we may trace the progress of this form, which also developed towards the pattern we now recognize during the seventeenth century.

The Bible, especially the Books of the Old Testament, is an anthology of vivid stories. From time immemorial artists (including the preachers to whom sermonizing was an art in itself) have taken delight in retelling, or painting, or carving these stories—often with the hope of emphasizing the morals which may be drawn from them. Illuminated manuscripts, mural paintings, and sculpture of the Middle Ages are a testimony to this, as also the religious drama of miracle and mystery and passion and nativity play in which all the arts met. In medieval drama music exerted a strong influence because it possessed a more "unearthly" or spiritual quality—for reasons developed in Chapter 1. The music itself hovered between "sacred" and "secular"; so long as it was dramatically apt no one complained.

During the sixteenth century this tradition was joined by the newer principles of Renaissance art. St. Philip Neri, the Roman saint, encouraged musico-dramatic performances based on religious themes in his Oratory (from which name comes the term *oratorio*), and before long such performances were of similar structure and character to opera. The first of the oratorios to be recognized as such is *La rappresentazione di anima e di corpo* ("The Representation of Soul and Body"), by Emilio de' Cavalieri, which was given in the church founded by St. Philip Neri in Rome. Cavalieri, who had lived in Florence where he had become acquainted with the ideas of the pioneers of opera, was not afraid to make this work attractive. He employed an orchestra similar to that used by Monteverdi in *Orfeo* and introduced a chorus. Moreover he insisted on his singers delivering their parts with due regard to expression.

Oratorio became almost as fashionable as opera in the Italian cities, and of the composers responsible for its development the most notable were Giacomo Carissimi and Alessandro Stradella. The former, who was also a master of the early cantata, was choirmaster first in Assisi, the town of St. Francis, and then in Rome. Some of his oratorios, with recitatives, airs, and choruses, are still occasionally to be heard. The best-known, and most effective, is *Jephtha*, from which Handel borrowed a complete chorus for the movement "Hear, Jacob's God" in *Samson*.

Stradella, whose present life was as adventurous and irregular as those of many of his contemporaries, also composed works which came to the notice of Handel. Of his oratorios the most popular was *St. John the Baptist*.

Italian oratorio, the tradition being carried on by Alessandro Scarlatti and Antonio Vivaldi, was brilliant, accomplished, colourful, and immediately effective. It belonged to the church, but also to the palace, for often such performances were given in the houses of the princes of the Church.

Across Europe, however, another and a violently contrasted type of religious musical art was moving towards a climax: the Passion setting. This, as we have discovered, also emerged from medieval drama, but in the sixteenth and seventeenth centuries it passed through the hands of people affected by religious divisions and a major war—the Thirty Years War (1618–48). The composer who did most to establish the Passion setting was Heinrich Schütz.

Schütz, whose life from 1585 to 1672 spanned the most revolutionary period in musical history, is one of the great figures of music. Like William Byrd he is best understood in relation to his environment, for he is as characteristically Saxon in attitude as Byrd is English, and his mode of expression is deeply rooted in the traditions of his country. Schütz also resembles Byrd—and his great successor, Bach—in appearing indifferent to success or failure, and in concentrating on the finest intellectual honesty in his craftsmanship.

Schütz was sent to Venice as a young man and he became accomplished in the composition of madrigals, motets, and "sacred symphonies", in which voices and instruments met on equal terms. He also took an interest in the new dramatic music and wrote an opera *Dafne* (the score of which was lost) for performance in Germany.

Schütz conducting his choir, from Christoph Bernhard's Geistliches
Gesang-Buch, *1676*

Schütz returned from Italy to Kassel (where a street is named in his honour), whence he moved to Dresden, as court musician. There he spent the remainder of his life, except for some years during the Thirty Years War, when life in Saxony was grievously upset. During this period he lived in Copenhagen.

Schütz was a fertile composer, but most of his genius was expended on religious music. He compiled a set of Psalms for use in the Electoral Chapel which were intended as a Lutheran counterpart to the psalter of the Calvinists. In 1645 he wrote a setting of the *Seven Words from the Cross* which was characterized by its solemnity and a simple dignity. In 1648 he affirmed his belief in the spiritual importance of German traditional style, as opposed to the new Italian, and issued a series of motets under the heading of *Geistliche Chormusik* ("Spiritual Choral Music"). Towards the end of his life he produced at least three settings of the *Passion*, of which the most important is that after the Gospel of St. Matthew. In this work, which is austerely unaccompanied, the narrative (which in Italian music is given in recitative) is delivered in a kind of plainsong. Otherwise the work consists of choruses, some of which are dramatic, and some reflective.

But Schütz was a composer of imagination, and his *Christmas Story* is as gay and varied in colour as the *Passion* according to St. Matthew is solemn and reflective.

German music in general may be described as expressive —that is, expressive of deep emotions and profound ideas. Italian music is, perhaps, more free, more melodic, more superficially descriptive; perhaps more immediately *musical*.

Often the German and the Italian traditions meet, as was the case with Schütz, and also with two other Saxon composers born thirteen years after his death in 1685.

7

Saxon and Anglo-Saxon

UNTIL the end of the seventeenth century the acknowledged great masters of music, whether composers of secular or religious works, were within the
Catholic tradition. An exception might be made of some
English musicians, particularly Henry Purcell, but even in
these cases it would be difficult to deny the influence of
those positive doctrines of Catholicism that still maintained the Church of England as an institution of compromise. In the first half of the eighteenth century, on the
other hand, music was dominated by two men, born in
the same year in neighbouring towns in Saxony, who were
brought up within a different tradition. They were George
Frideric Handel (as he was to sign his name in England)
and Johann Sebastian Bach; the year of their birth was
1685.

Saxony was the land of Martin Luther, and Protestant-
ism quickly established itself there. When Bach and
Handel were boys the ancient churches of Saxony had
mostly been Lutheran or Calvinist for many years.
Handel's grandfather, indeed, was a Lutheran pastor in
the little church charmingly poised over the river Saale
and facing the ancient castle of Giebichenstein, a suburb
of the city of Halle where the Handel family lived. Handel
was christened in the Lutheran Market Church of Halle
and he went to a Lutheran school and university. As a

The Thomaskirche, Leipzig

young man he gained a more intimate knowledge of the
other prevailing Protestant influence when he became, for
a brief period, organist of the Calvinist cathedral in Halle.

Bach was a native of Eisenach, beside which rises the
Wartburg where Luther had been imprisoned. He too was
educated under Lutheran influence, and for the greater
part of his life he was associated with that faith as chorister
and organist. For the last twenty-seven years of his life he
was Cantor at St. Thomas's in Leipzig, perhaps the most
important church foundation in Saxony.

First impressions and influences are ineradicable. That Bach never escaped from the climate of Lutheran thought is hardly surprising, for he stayed at home, working always in his native province. In the case of Handel, who left Halle as a young man and spent the greater part of his working life in England, the forces which fashioned his youth became more diffused and, therefore, more difficult to analyse. However, the fact that he made of oratorio a medium which later was accepted by English Protestants as a particular and meaningful means of expression is not, perhaps, entirely accidental. On a simpler level it is interesting to note that his pronunciation of English, as given by Dr. Burney who knew him, shows the same transposition of "b's" and "p's" that characterizes Saxon dialect even today.

The focal works of Bach's great output are his church cantatas and his settings of the Passion, especially those according to St. John and St. Matthew. In these is summarized the attitude to worship of his fellow-countrymen, just as the Catholic attitude is in the masses and motets of the fifteenth and sixteenth centuries. Handel also composed two Passions—not, however, among his most notable achievements—which relate to his German interests. But neither composer was restricted to religious music; in each case this was but one aspect among many.

The eighteenth century was an age in which men had wide interests. Germany was a land divided into princedoms and dukedoms, and each regional ruler maintained a court wherein the arts and other intellectual interests were generally cultivated. Secular music, particularly for instruments, was in high favour. Bach and Handel had many opportunities in that sphere. Bach was organist and chamber musician at Weimar between 1708 and 1717, and in charge of the chamber music at the court of Cöthen for the next six years. Handel had acquaintance with the court at Weissenfels, where his father attended as surgeon, when he was a boy, and after a three-year visit to Italy he was attached to the Electoral Court at Hanover until he came to live permanently in England.

Bach and Handel thus had opportunity to compose a variety of music, and between them they covered every form practised in the first half of the eighteenth century. As their commitments were different, and their respective audiences generally looked for somewhat different values, their modes of expression were inevitably also different. That, in general, we recognize the style of Bach and the style of Handel as separate is due not only to different personal aptitudes and characteristics but also to the effect on them of the communities in which they worked. Music, whether folk-music or art-music, is to some degree always a combined effort.

The most familiar keyboard music of Bach is the set of 48 Preludes and Fugues for "Well-tempered Clavier", the Preludes and Fugues for organ, the Chorale Preludes, and the Suites. In composing preludes and fugues—whether for harpsichord or for organ—Bach was following a familiar design. The works which he often took as models were by Froberger, Johann Pachelbel, who also worked in Saxony, and Dietrich Buxtehude, of Lübeck, and Kuhnau. Bach took what was best in each musical style and incorporated it within his own technique. But his mind ranged further. He had not only an æsthetic but also a scientific concern for music, which led him to appreciate the significance of the new system of "equal temperament" tuning. This, already applied to composition by the Baden musician Johann Fischer, gave to the composer opportunity to use freely all the major and minor keys, and easily to pass from one to another in the course of the same

Johann Sebastian Bach

piece. Bach's acceptance of the system was signalized by the 48 Preludes and Fugues; but all his music shows the infinite harmonic possibilities of music, particularly in regard to emotional expression.

Bach's scientific attitude reached its climax in the two great works of his last years, *A Musical Offering* and the *Art of Fugue*, both of which represent his intense concern for the intellectual structure of music, but also the interest of Frederick the Great, of Prussia, whose summoning of the composer to Potsdam was a highlight of Bach's last years.

In Bach's keyboard music a care for detail is always

evident, especially in the chorale preludes in which there is a great deal of minute description of textual points. There are many other elements. In the large-scale fantasias, toccatas, and preludes, there is a great exuberance. These show the great performer's desire to demonstrate his skill —and Bach was noted more in his own day as executant than as composer—and also effectively parallel the extravagances and boldness of contemporary baroque art in other fields. At another extreme there are simple teaching pieces, as for instance in the Anna Magdalena Music Book.

Although Bach lived in the relative seclusion of Saxony he studied music from other lands avidly. So his *French Suites* reflect something of the poise and brilliance of the French school of writers for harpsichord which had lately come to a glorious harvest in the works of François Couperin. These were published in four books, in 1713, 1716, 1722, and 1730. Another deservedly popular work by Bach is the *Italian Concerto*, which acknowledges the instrumental style developed especially by Antonio Vivaldi of Venice.

The Italian influence permeated much of Bach's output. His recitatives and arias are German variants on Italian style; but most of all is the Italian manner to be appreciated in his concertos. Indeed he went so far as to appropriate concertos (originally for violin) by Vivaldi and to rearrange them for harpsichord and string ensemble. The *Brandenburg Concertos* of 1721 are, in fact, *concerti grossi* planned for the instrumentalists available to Bach at the time, for when he composed them he was in the service of the court at Cöthen. In the scores of Bach a number of instruments appear which are now obsolete, such as *violino piccolo, viola d'amore, violoncello piccolo, oboe d'amore,* and *oboe da caccia.*

In the works of Handel roughly parallel to those of Bach which have so far been discussed there are both similarities and differences. Handel composed relatively little keyboard music, but his fugues and suites (which are grievously overlooked by performers today) have a frequent stolidity of purpose that at times brings them near to the art of Bach. In variations, however, he would appear to have been more concerned with the needs of the moment (to produce an effective display piece) than with any idea of "art for art's sake". So far as the solo concerto was concerned Handel—not so happily placed as was Bach with his university musical society in Leipzig—limited himself to organ concertos, one of which was also designated for the harp. These, which also stem from Italian concerto, were pioneer works, written more often than not for performance by the composer between the acts of the oratorios, and are of great variety and beauty. They were composed for the small, bright-voiced, chamber organ which was used in the theatres where oratorios were given.

By the side of Bach's *Brandenburg Concertos* may be placed Handel's *concerti grossi* (at least eighteen of which are in the general repertoire) and the more loosely constructed *Water Music* and *Music for the Royal Fireworks*. Broadly speaking these works stem from Corelli, whom Handel knew well in the early years of the century, and are clear and economical in utterance. All in all they possess a "public" quality in contrast to the more "private" nature of comparable works by Bach. They were, as was appreciated, rather more precisely within the fashionable idiom of the day as it was universally understood.

At this point we reach the essential difference between the two masters. Handel lived in the public eye; Bach did not. The former moved easily in different parts of

Handel, from a portrait by William Hogarth

Germany, Italy and England; was at ease in all sorts of
societies; and quickly absorbed the spirit of the place in
which he was at the time living. Bach stayed at home.
Handel loved the theatre, as Bach the church.

By the beginning of the eighteenth century Italian opera
had conquered Europe and every young man who aspired

to being a successful composer worked in this exciting medium. An opera was a string of recitatives and arias, occasionally interspersed with duets and other concerted numbers, brief orchestral pieces normally entitled "symphonies", and prefaced by an overture. An opera might or might not be dramatic: it must be tuneful—a vehicle for the skill of the Italian singers who overran Europe. Handel won success in Italy when his *Agrippina* was acclaimed in Venice at the end of 1709. Two years later Handel produced his first opera, *Rinaldo*, in London. After journeying between England and Hanover (where officially he was employed) Handel returned to London in 1712 for the production of *Il pastor fido* at the King's Theatre in the Haymarket.

Opera followed opera until there were in the end some forty of them from Handel's pen. Some were successful, some were not. On occasion singers were awkward, or audiences stayed away for reasons not always connected with music. Handel made money, and lost money. Overall he achieved great fame, not least of all because his melodies, published separately by the shrewd John Walsh, were so immediately attractive.

There is, however, more to it than this. Handel's operas frequently showed magnificent characterization and scene-painting in terms of music, and a balance and finish astonishing in view of the generally hurried manner in which they were put together. Among the first of the operas are *Giulio Cesare* (with wonderful orchestral effects), *Ariodante* (with a *corps de ballet*), *Orlando* (in which the composer experiments with unusual time signatures), and *Poro*. Rarely performed in England, these works are happily restored to the repertoire of some of the leading German opera houses, especially that of Handel's birthplace—Halle.

Although Handel continued to compose operas until 1742 the form went out of favour in England many years earlier. A convenient date to remember is 1728, for in that year an opera in English—the *Beggar's Opera*—achieved enormous success. This was satisfactory to those who did not like Italian singers, who were frequently both temperamental and opinionated; to those who could not understand Italian; to those who considered English as satisfactory for musical purposes as Italian; and to those who preferred "real life" on the stage to representations of heroes of antiquity.

Handel met the situation with characteristic common sense. He transferred his operatic technique to the already existing form of oratorio, in which English words of a generally religious significance were now employed. The oratorios were performed in the theatre, and they differed from opera only

The German flautist Wiedman and the singer Giovanni Carestini: detail of engraving of scene from Hogarth's "Marriage à la Mode"

in that no acting took place. Handel's first oratorio (not so called) had been produced in 1720, privately, at the palace of the Duke of Chandos at Cannons in Middlesex. This was revived in 1732, and thereafter oratorios came regularly until 1752, in which year Handel's eyesight gave him great trouble.

The oratorios were similar to opera except in one important respect; more and more the chorus came to play a major part, either to comment on the action from without (as the "chorus" in Greek drama) or to participate in it. Here Handel joined his early experience of German music with that gained in writing anthems in England. It is the great choruses, such as those particularly in *Messiah*, *Israel in Egypt*, and *Judas Maccabæus*, which quickly gained the affection of English singers both in London and the provinces.

The oratorios of Handel, and the cantatas and Passions of Bach, were written for small choirs of boys and men, and for relatively small orchestras with strings, oboes, bassoons, and harpsichords as the mainstay, and additional trumpets, drums, and so on, for details of colour. In using these forces, however, the composers were guided by different principles. Handel was concerned with conveying his ideas—what he thought about his characters and the situations in which they were placed—to the "general public", often fickle, incalculable, and waywardly critical, and able to register disapproval by refusing to support the composer's projects, and thereby affecting his livelihood. Bach had a captive audience, of those who attended church as a matter of course. To the worthy Leipzigers who went to St. Thomas's Church the moments of anguish and drama and the involved contrapuntal texture of the style shown in the *St. Matthew Passion* must have been often perplexing. Forward-looking music critics in the city sometimes suggested that Bach was old-fashioned. But Bach, secure in his official position, was able to be indifferent to praise or censure, and to continue to write for "the greater glory of God".

It is, however, easy to misunderstand the situation. It cannot be proved—indeed the evidence is weighted against such a conclusion—that Bach was more religious than Handel, only that he approached the composition of music which relied on religious texts from a different angle. That this was so was in large measure a matter of environment and opportunity.

Bach and Handel were not the only composers of their generation, though few others have exercised anything like the same influence on the music and thought of later times. One contemporary musician to stand apart in individual eminence is Domenico Scarlatti. He, son of Alessandro Scarlatti of Naples, was the great harpsichord virtuoso of the eighteenth century, and in his sonatas is enshrined his regard for the more poetical virtues of his instrument. As later was Chopin to the pianoforte, so, a century earlier, was Domenico Scarlatti to the harpsichord. His fame in his lifetime was considerable and he travelled widely, performing in England, Portugal, and Spain, where he spent many years.

From his father Domenico Scarlatti inherited a great love of melody and reservations regarding the high priority set on contrapuntal writing by so many composers of the baroque era. Reaction against "heavy" music set in fairly early (Handel enjoyed the best of both worlds), and while Bach was composing his masterpieces George Philipp Telemann—yet another Saxon, born in Magdeburg—was enjoying a more enthusiastic reception on account of his cultivation of a lighter manner of writing. Telemann wrote a vast amount of music, including 600 suites and about 40 each of operas and Passions, and some of it has recently enjoyed revival. The reason for this is that Telemann's fluent music is agreeable to amateur ensembles who wish to avoid disaster at the high hurdles provided by greater composers; but it is not often memorable.

Telemann, however, deserves other commemoration, for he was a pioneer of the public concert in Germany, establishing series in Frankfurt in 1713, and in Hamburg in 1720. Five years later the famous *Concerts spirituels* were inaugurated in Paris.

From what has been so far said it is clear that during the age of Handel and Bach the orchestra won a position of independence and importance. Such a development meant that standards of virtuoso technique were likely to be fostered somewhere. This in fact happened at the Electoral Court of Mannheim, in the southern part of the valley of the Rhine.

Music played a large part in the life of the town of Mannheim and nearby Schwetzingen, where the court repaired for the summer, and of the 25,000 inhabitants not fewer than a hundred were expert singers and players, in addition to which there was a large resident body of pensioners from the Electoral music corps. The Elector himself was a flautist—like Frederick the Great—and also a 'cellist, and his interest and generosity encouraged musicians from far away. Among the strangers who came to Mannheim were the Bohemians Franz Richter and Johann Stamitz.

Stamitz, who was born in 1717 and died in 1757, lived within the lifetime of Handel, but he worked to a different end. Although, like every musician of the eighteenth century, he was versatile and composed in many different forms, his chief interest was in instrumental music. This is not surprising, for he was a remarkable performer on

135

every stringed instrument. Stamitz was especially interested in the Italian three-movement overtures, and the
solo concertos. He developed what is now conveniently
known as "sonata form"—the general design characteristic of "classical music"—and gave to symphony and
concerto a status encouraging to subsequent composers.
More than that, he chose his players carefully and trained
them to play together in a disciplined style. That is what
Corelli had done, and in so doing established the *concerto
grosso*. Thus we see that musical forms in themselves are
less important than the opportunity they afford for
expression.

The playing of the Mannheim orchestra, which maintained its high standard to the end of the century, was
almost sensational. "Their forte", wrote a contemporary
poet, "is like thunder, their crescendo a cataract, their
diminuendo the rippling of a crystal stream, their piano,
the soft breath of early spring." In the exploiting of these
dynamic effects the orchestra—in Dr. Burney's words—
discovered "musical *colours* which had their *shades*, as much
as red or blue in painting".

Colour in music, whether suggested by the contrasting
tone-qualities of instruments or voices, by the ebb and
flow of expression or by both, is a factor in musical
experience of the greatest importance. It is always present
as a memorial to the ineradicable impulse which is generally described as Romantic. Not even the most classical
and scientifically contrived music can live for long if it
lacks the vitality that comes from this impulse. The greater
the sense of humanism that prevails, the greater the attention to the expressive power and qualities of music. This,
perhaps, is the point at which the music of Handel departs
from that of Bach. Of the two composers Handel was the
more humanist, Bach the more consciously devoted to the

philosophy of a universe designed and ruled by God. In the eighteenth century that, as a general basis for philosophy and conduct, was out of date.

The music of the first half of the eighteenth century was dominated by Bach and Handel; the philosophy by the French sceptic Voltaire.

8

New Values

IN 1737 a Leipzig writer on music (musical journalism may be said to have been born in the eighteenth century) complained of Bach's music that it was thick, confused, "unnatural" and therefore artificial, and in conflict with Reason. Reason: that was the vogue word of the age to which it gave its name, and an indication of the feeling of self-sufficiency generally experienced. By reason, of course, was meant human reason.

Of those who tried to apply the principles of scientific inquiry and logic to music in the eighteenth century the most important was the French composer and theoretician Jean-Philippe Rameau. Although he was a successful composer of operas and ballets—in which he carried on many of the traditions of Lully—Rameau's fame depends on his *Traité de l'Harmonie*, published in 1722. In this he stated the principles of harmony that dominated musical thought until the end of the nineteenth century, and which to some extent are still in evidence. Rameau systematized the chords in common use; laid down the kinds of key-change, or modulation, that were possible according to "reason"; and reversed the generally held opinion that melody was more important than harmony by saying that "melody stems from harmony". The character of melodies for a century and a half after Rameau's exposition of his ideas shows how effective was his teaching.

Rameau not only discussed the physical nature of

music but also its wider implications and significance. For him, and for most of his contemporaries (and for many people at all times), music conveyed meaning. Particular melodic intervals, and particular keys, therefore, were suggested as appropriate to particular emotions and circumstances. Up to a point Rameau, like every theoretician aiming at order within art, was defining what was general practice; but the manner in which his conclusions were set seemed to give them greater authority, and their effect, finally, was constricting.

There were, however, other ideas generally held which needed stating and were beneficial. Lightness, elegance, formal precision and delicacy; these are virtues in art, and they were the qualities most appreciated in the era which succeeded to that of Bach and Handel. Dramatically, the changed outlook was expressed in music by Bach's own sons—none of whom appreciated much of the significance of their father's work.

Wilhelm Friedemann, the eldest, who spent twenty years as organist in Halle, was a tasteful and "delicate" executant on the clavier and a composer of symphonies and concertos in the new vein. The second son was Carl Philipp Emanuel, by far the most highly respected member of the family in the eighteenth century. For many years he was cembalist at the court of Frederick the Great, where his lively wit and quick intelligence made him a great favourite. His reported observations on music show him to have been a quick conversationalist with a keen awareness of the æsthetic values of the circle in which he moved. He was also a ready composer and left a great body of music of all sorts. His most important contributions were his sonatas and other pieces for clavier, which looked forward to, and served as models for, those of Haydn and Beethoven.

Wilhelm Friedemann and Carl Philipp Emanuel were sons of Bach's first marriage; Johann Christian, the youngest of his children and twenty-one years junior to Carl Philipp Emanuel, of the second—to Anna Magdalena. Johann Christian lived with his Berlin brother after their father's death, and then, being both restless and ambitious, went to Italy. There his success was similar to that of Handel at an earlier period. He was widely applauded because he was able to write, with compelling ease, in the current, suave, Italian manner. He lived in Milan for a time, as organist of the cathedral, but in 1762 migrated to England.

In London the youngest of the Bachs became music master to the Queen, and a promoter of public subscription concerts, for which he composed numerous symphonies. These are characterized by great melodic charm and by a refined manner of orchestration. In his early symphonies Johann Christian indicated a part for the harpsichord; in the later ones this was not the case. Thus we note a future step in the emancipation of the orchestra as a complete and self-contained unit.

In 1764 an eight-year-old boy prodigy from Austria (with his gifted sister and proud father) was visiting London: Wolfgang Amadeus Mozart. The boy was introduced to Bach and was impressed by his kindness and interest. He was still more impressed by what he was able to hear of the music. He went back to Austria well-versed in the symphonic art of J. C. Bach, and took that master as one of his earliest models.

Carl Philipp Emanuel Bach once passed this opinion on his father: "He did not have the most brilliant good fortune because he did not do the one thing that is really essential, that is, roam about the world." This may be put in another way by saying that to be successful in the eighteenth century it was necessary to give the appearance of being a man-of-the-world. Many composers, as had Handel, moved from country to country carrying with them the international currency of Italian opera. J. C. Bach himself is a case in point. His skill in this art-form gave him the entrée to many cities, and he was invited to compose operas in Turin, Florence, Naples, Paris, Mannheim, and London.

Operas in the eighteenth century were, for the most part, written according to a set plan which did not give great scope for individuality. Whether an opera was by Buononcini, or Jommelli, or Porpora, or Hasse, or J. C. Bach (all being distinguished composers) mattered little. So long as the arias, in A B A pattern, were aptly "pathetic", "heroic", and tuneful, nothing else was considered important. The intentions of the Florentine pioneers of 1600 had miscarried and opera had hardened into a rigid set of conventions. Composers, whether they realized it or not, were dominated by brilliant, often arrogant, singers and by a public that knew what it liked and was determined to have it.

The main form of opera was described as *opera seria*, of which the subjects were always taken from "heroic" and classical sources. The writing of libretti was a constant employment for poets and by far the most celebrated librettist was Pietro Trapassi, known as Metastasio, who was born in Rome in 1698 and lived on until 1782. Metastasio's reputation was such that in 1729 he was appointed court poet in Vienna, where he lived until his death. Musicians associated with him at different times included Caldara, Pergolesi, J. C. Bach, Handel, Gluck, Graun, Hasse, Jommelli, Leo and Mozart.

Of these composers two are immediately important—Pergolesi and Gluck.

Pergolesi was one of the first masters of comic opera, or *opera buffa* as it was called. *Opera seria* was fashionable all over Europe, but even in Italy audiences found the repetition of ancient stories somewhat monotonous, however fine the performance of singers and instrumentalists. Therefore the directors of the opera houses relieved the general pattern by inserting comic interludes or *intermezzi* between the acts.

Pergolesi's most famous *opera buffa* was *La serva padrona*, which grew into an independent work after first having been composed as an intermezzo. Thereafter *opera seria* and *opera buffa* lived side by side, the latter exerting its influence in favour of drama rather than of mere vocal display. When Pergolesi's *Serva padrona* was performed in Paris in 1752 it created a sensation, and the Italian players who produced it began a controversy which split French society. There were those in this *Guerre des Bouffons* who protested that Italian opera was superior to French, being more rational and less complicated, and those who considered the works of

Character from Italian comedy, painted on an Italian maiolica plate, c. 1760

Lully and Rameau to be truer to traditional French dramatic values. Supporters of French opera sat on the King's side in the theatre, their opponents on that of the Queen. (As in many such controversies, personal, political, and national questions of the day were the real issues, which could then conveniently be symbolized in terms of opera.)

The upshot was that French composers derived much from the example of *opera buffa* and developed their own *opéra comique*.

The success of *opera buffa* was one result of antagonism to *opera seria*. In England and France ballad opera represented another. In Germany there was an independent

Gluck's " Orpheus", adapted from the title-page

and popular entertainment of similar character known as *Singspiel*, and in Spain the native *zarzuela*. These forms derived from older traditions which reached back to the Middle Ages, and from folk-song. The artificiality of opera was, however, most powerfully assailed by Gluck, one of the outstanding figures of eighteenth-century music. Gluck was of Bohemian-German origin, and in early life he achieved great success in Italy. From Italy he went to London where he arrived in time for the Stuart rising of 1745, which affected adversely the reception given to foreign visitors; thus Gluck made little impression there. As was the general practice with such composers he then went from one European city to another, and in 1762 produced *Orfeo e Euridice* in Vienna. The libretto was by Ranieri da Calzabigi, who was anxious to develop the dramatic quality of opera, and in Gluck he found a willing collaborator. In the introduction to a later opera, *Alceste*, Gluck expressed his point of view—which was not far removed from that of the earlier Florentines, but far distant from that of his contemporaries.

"It was my intention", wrote the composer,

> to strip music of the abuses by which it has been disfigured by vain singers and complacent composers. I wanted to keep music to its proper operatic purposes, of helping the expression of the story without stopping the action simply for the sake of superfluous ornaments. It seems to me that when music is joined to poetry it is like colour in a picture, where light and shade give life to figures without destroying their outline.
>
> As for the overture, this should give the audience some idea of the forthcoming action, while instrumental accompaniment should be regulated entirely by dramatic considerations.
>
> My first duty, however, has been to aim at a noble simplicity.

Gluck spent much of his life in Vienna and owed much to the encouragement of the Viennese.

During the eighteenth century Vienna became the virtual capital of European music, the result of a generous cultivation of all forms of music and the reception of musicians from many lands over a long period of years. Rulers such as Leopold I and Joseph I were not only patrons of the art but also practising composers. During the reign of the former some 400 Italian operas were performed in Vienna, while Joseph I built new theatres and increased the royal staff of musicians. His successor, Charles VI, encouraged oratorios and masses, composed in colourful baroque style to match the new glories of Viennese architecture, as well as operas and instrumental music. The War of Austrian Succession that followed on the accession of Maria Theresa hindered progress in some respects, but the love of music was too strongly ingrained both in court and city for its development to be altogether stifled. There was, in fact, a flowering of instrumental music, no longer in the baroque idiom but more slender, graceful, and *galant*, with some of the properties that in the other arts are described as rococo. For the young musician there were many opportunities in Vienna, for a love of music was characteristic of social life at every level.

At about the time of Johann Sebastian Bach's death one such young musician, having just left the cathedral choir, was thrown upon his own resources in Vienna. He was Josef Haydn. His first real opportunity came when he met Karl Joseph von Fürnberg, a wealthy amateur, who was in the habit of holding musical house-parties at his country estate of Weinzierl. As was customary in such a household, members of the staff were often practising musicians. When Haydn submitted his compositions, therefore, they were played by an ensemble which included the pastor of the parish, the steward, and a couple of huntsmen (whose horns served a double purpose) from the estate staff. Haydn composed a variety of music for this patron, which was of some significance, for the string quartet and the symphony began to emerge in their own right.

The balance of four stringed instruments, whose individual importance was soon to become equal, was a minor revolution. Until Haydn took steps in this direction the

The viola arrives

trio of two violins and 'cello—with harpsichord to supply a complete chordal complement—was the principal vehicle of chamber music, while in orchestral writing the tendency had been to ignore the possibilities of the viola— an instrument given only to bad violinists. In the course of his life Haydn composed some eighty quartets, among them some of the noblest pieces in this class, which were models for all subsequent composers of chamber music. His devotion to the medium was encouraged in the first place by his friends at Weinzierl. While he was there he also composed his earliest symphonies, which, like the quartets and piano sonatas, followed the structural designs of C. P. E. Bach. The number of movements in the works varied, but by 1756 the pattern of quick movement, slow movement, minuet, and finale was regularized.

The symphonies grew out of the entertainment music which was required at frequent intervals, and which was described variously as divertimento, cassation, nocturne, or serenade.

Haydn was not only a fine musician but an agreeable person, and well able to accept the role of servant which patronage of that era imposed. He was recommended to Count Ferdinand Morzin, who had a private orchestra of a dozen or so players, and after two pleasant and prolific years as his music director Haydn was appointed Kapell-meister to the Prince Esterházy, who spent his time be-tween his country estates, first at Eisenstadt, later at Esterház, and Vienna.

Haydn was in the service of the Esterházy family from 1761 until his death in 1809. This was a crucial period in the history of music, for it witnessed a complete change of emphasis in the art. Music freed itself finally from the powerful influence of religion and reached its highest point in independence; for the mature symphony or string quartet of Haydn, and even more of Mozart, was reckoned valuable for itself alone. It was not there to support, or to express, the liturgy of the church, nor to carry the libretto of an opera: it was abstract. So far as audiences were concerned they enjoyed music for its own sake, reading into it meanings which were purely personal and not provided in advance for them. The growth in popularity of symphonic music was general and its cultivation in the public concert-rooms of Europe brought music as a recreational activity to many whose opportunities had previously been more limited.

Haydn wrote many symphonies for the court at Esterház, but their wider use was made possible by the publication of some of them by the Viennese publisher Artaria. A set of six symphonies, including those known as "La Poule" and "La Reine", were commissioned by a musical society in Paris and are, therefore, known as the "Paris" symphonies. Twelve later symphonies, composed during the last decade of the eighteenth century, were composed for the London concert promoter, Johann Salomon. Haydn himself visited London, first in 1790, and secondly in 1794, to take part in the performance of his "London" symphonies, among which are those familiarly known as the "Surprise", the "Clock", and the "Drum-roll".

Within the duration of the mature career of Haydn was the whole lifetime of Mozart, who was born in 1756—by which time Haydn had composed his first string quartets; and died in 1791—before the older master had begun many of the works by which he is now best known.

Mozart wrote about fifty symphonies, of which the last three, composed in 1788, are the most finished and impressive. Mozart's style owed much to the Italian music which he had studied, but his symphonies and chamber music especially showed how much he also owed to Josef Haydn. In a sense the two composers were interdependent, for Haydn, despite his seniority, was always ready to acknowledge the genius of Mozart and never too proud to benefit from its manifestations.

The general pattern of the symphony as it was left by Mozart and Haydn was as follows: slow introduction, which had especially been introduced and developed by Haydn and then adopted by Mozart, running into the main body of the first movement; this, like the earlier Italian overtures from which it was derived, was in quick time and characterized by two contrasting groups of themes which were stated, developed, and restated; slow movement, of a song-like character and not unassociated with the aria, which might formally relate to the "sonata" structure of the first movement or else be a set of "air and variations"; minuet, descended from the seventeenth-century suites, and passed into symphony by way of the lighter divertimento and serenade; finale, frequently in the shape of a gay rondo (A B A C A D . . . etc.) but developed into more subtle forms by Mozart, as in the "Jupiter" symphony. The orchestra involved included, by the end of the century, two each of flutes, oboes, clarinets (the last instruments to arrive in the "symphony" orchestra), bassoons, horns, trumpets, and drums; with strings.

Throughout the eighteenth century a keyboard instrument was obligatory in orchestral music, but by the end of the century it no longer fulfilled an indispensable part. The orchestra was a balanced unit in itself.

As for the keyboard instrument, this by now was not what it had been. The instrument of Handel and Bach was the harpsichord; of Haydn, in later life, and Mozart, the *pianoforte*, or *forte piano* as it was then called. This instrument was developed in Germany and then in England by workmen driven out of Germany through the wars of the eighteenth century. Famous makers of pianofortes in the eighteenth century were Gottfried Silbermann, the organ builder of Freiburg; his pupil Johann Zampe, who worked in London, and his son-in-law, and sometime apprentice, John Broadwood. The Austrian manufacturers Stein and Streicher (Stein's son-in-law) made instruments with a lighter touch than the German or the English, and theirs were the pianofortes with which Mozart was most familiar. In Paris a great contribution to the art of piano-making was that of Sebastian Erard.

It was left to composers of the nineteenth century to realize the full possibilities of the pianoforte, but the keyboard sonatas of Haydn and Mozart—extensive, and constructed in the same manner as symphonies—and more particularly the concertos of the latter, showed new and exciting ranges of tone-colour. The solo concertos of Haydn and Mozart (Mozart, a virtuoso performer himself, is more conspicuous in this field) differ from those of their predecessors both in respect of design (the late eighteenth-century concerto was as a symphony in form but without a minuet) and in tonal valuation. In Bach and Vivaldi the listener is aware of incisive lines of sound, in Mozart of subtle melodies set against an enchanting kaleidoscope of varying masses of instrumental tone, now string, now woodwind. The invariable first impression, therefore, is of grace and charm, qualities which stand prominent in music of the "classical" period.

Music, however, is fluid: it is never merely this to the exclusion of that. Changes which appear clear-cut in retrospect never seem so at the time, so that one may easily live through an artistic revolution without noticing it. That is evident in the music of our own day: the popular music of today is different from that of yesterday, although we rarely know why or how; the same is true of more serious music, and of the music of earlier generations.

Josef Haydn grew up to accept the obligations imposed on a creative musician by the society in which he lived. According to age-old tradition he supplied masses for the court chapel, symphonies, chamber music, and operas of rather local appeal, for secular entertainment, much as a provision merchant would supply groceries. There is, of course, something attractive about the selfless artist thus adding grace and beauty to the life of the community; but the portrait of Haydn is not quite so simple as that. At some stage in his career his music became a dominating factor in the cultural life of England. The servant became greater than his master, and Haydn, not the Prince Ester-házy, acquired universal fame and respect. That this was so was due to the quality of the music—not the personal ambition of the composer—and the music changed imperceptibly, gaining in power from experience.

Haydn was curious. He explored folk-music so that his most "classical" symphonies show the influence of the folk-songs with which he was familiar. He thrilled to the infinite variety of tone-colours to be produced by the instruments in use in the eighteenth century. Therefore his scores became progressively richer, culminating in the spacious canvasses of such works as the symphonies and unjustly neglected masses, written towards the end of the century, and *The Creation*. These, because of their wealth of colour and occasional reference to ideas lying outside the field of "abstract" music, are properly considered to show a Romantic impulse.

The truth is that Haydn was always inclined to a romantic outlook. His symphonies and quartets, for

"The Creation", a fresco by Michelangelo in the Sistine Chapel, Rome

example, often carry sub-titles and are, to a point, sometimes descriptive. The descriptiveness of, say, the "Lark" Quartet, the "Bear" Symphony, or the "Clock" Symphony is, however, superficial and incidental to the design of the music. We may therefore feel inclined to say that with a few exceptions in his last years Haydn's art lacked emotion—though this depends on one's personal point of view. Taking that a stage further, we do not feel the impress of Haydn's emotions on his music, which is ever well-bred and considerate to the audience.

Mozart, twenty years junior to Haydn, had a different temperament and led a different sort of life. He was a child prodigy, exploited by his father and at first pampered by society, who found it difficult to settle down to the humdrum life of an eighteenth-century Austrian musician. Dissatisfaction bred discontent, and awareness of his own great gifts made Mozart critical of the social scene. The record of Mozart's innermost feelings is in his published letters.

Mozart was what would now be called an "angry young

man"; as a servant of the unpopular Archbishop of Salzburg, he had good reason. In the early summer of 1781 Mozart, whose reputation stood high in musical circles in Vienna, was subject to the worst possible treatment. "The Archbishop", he wrote to his father, "runs me down to everyone here and has not the sense to see that such a proceeding does him no credit; for I am more highly respected in Vienna than he is. He is only known as a presumptuous conceited ecclesiastic, who despises everyone here, whereas I am considered a very amiable person. It is true that I have become proud when I see that someone is trying to treat me with contempt and *en bagatelle*; and that is the way in which the Archbishop invariably treats me; whereas by kind words he could make me do as he pleased." The end of Mozart's career as musician to the Archbishop came shortly afterwards. He was, literally, kicked out of office.

Recognizing his own value to the community, Mozart composed incessantly. His works depended on patronage, and frequently he was obliged to cultivate the influential, but they—however self-important—must know their place. Thus he wrote to his father in the summer of 1782:

> The Viennese gentry, and in particular the Emperor, must not imagine that I am on this earth solely for the sake of Vienna. There is no monarch in the world whom I should be more glad to serve than the Emperor, but I refuse to beg for my post. I believe that I am capable of doing credit to any court. If Germany, my beloved fatherland, of which, as you know, I am proud, will not accept me, then in God's name let France or England become the richer by another talented German, to the disgrace of the German nation.

From these, and other, excerpts, it may be deduced that Mozart, although ready enough to seek patronage and to applaud the enlightened and encouraging patron, felt that his own exceptional gifts entitled him to a respect equal to that accorded to those who were enjoying great privileges through no exceptional merit of their own. It is also clear that Mozart saw himself as of national significance.

The philosophy of the Renaissance had encouraged humanism in a general way. The teaching of Voltaire stimulated rationalism and scepticism, and a mistrust of arbitrary authority. During the lifetime of Haydn and Mozart the voice of Jean-Jacques Rousseau was powerful, passionately exalting the importance of the individual and giving a new meaning to what now would be described as the subconscious parts of personality. At the same time German literature was being made into a vital national

From a porcelain figure modelled by Johann Christian William Beyer at Ludwigsburg, c. 1765

and international force by Goethe, poet, philosopher, and dramatist, who from 1775 lived in an honoured position at the court of Weimar, and also by Schiller. Both Goethe and Schiller were artists of epic stature, on whom a large part of the cultural tradition of nineteenth-century Germany was built.

To what extent Mozart was directly influenced by his great contemporaries in other fields is, and must remain, uncertain, but the idea that as a great musician he was detached from and unaware of tendencies in art, politics, and religion is false. On the one hand are his letters, on the other the record of the books of poetry, general literature, and philosophy that comprised his library.

When we look for a connection between the impulses of the age and his music we can be guided by the nature of the music, and by the relationship between words and music in those works which spring from verbal concepts.

Mozart lived in the eighteenth century and was, therefore, obliged to address his audiences in terms which they understood. Hence the patterning of his music, according to the same accepted formal principles as were enunciated also by Haydn, Pleyel, Dittersdorf, Gyrowetz, Gossec, and half a hundred other busy composers, is lucid and readily to be comprehended. So, too, with rare exceptions (as the perplexing introduction to the so-called "Dissonance" quartet in C major, K.465) is the syntax of the music. The clarity of style is sometimes taken as an end in itself, with the result that the superficial "beauty" of the music is exaggerated at the expense of its inner meaning.

What is "meaning"? In Mozart's instrumental music this is sensed from the contrast of themes, as, for example, in the G minor and C major symphonies of 1788, which are not unrelated to the shape of operatic melodies; in the subtle interplay of harmonies and key-relationships, and

155

the choice of keys and chords, as with the piano concertos in A major (K.488) and C minor (K.491); in the appraisal of instrumental characteristics which led to the composition of the clarinet concerto and the significant contribution made by that instrument to the E flat symphony of 1788.

Mozart's chamber music, symphonies, sonatas, and concertos give no romantic suggestions in their titles, and do not express the composer's moods of the moment. Thus they are abstract. On the other hand they compel attention by their clear emotional implications. By these we gain insight into character, not necessarily Mozart's character, but rather that of mankind in general. Whether this is the proper function of music, whether music indeed is able to undertake such a function at all, is arguable—and there are powerful arguments to the contrary, particularly put forward in our own time by Igor Stravinsky; but that it was so was firmly believed by musicians of the generation that succeeded that of Haydn and Mozart, and they based their own musical expression on this belief. They were much affected by the operas of Mozart.

Mozart was one of the greatest, some might say the greatest, of all opera composers. His works in this genre form a unique body of masterpieces of contrasted kinds, superbly balanced, touching all previously familiar traditions of operatic technique, and universally accepted.

In 1768, Mozart, then a boy of twelve, composed *Bastien and Bastienne* (in the overture to which may be heard the opening theme of the first movement of Beethoven's "Eroica" symphony), at the request of Dr. Anton Mesmer of Vienna. In *Bastien and Bastienne* Mozart combined the styles of French comic opera and German *Singspiel*. *The Marriage of Figaro, Don Giovanni*, and *Cosi fan tutte*—all to libretti by Lorenzo da Ponte, the next great librettist after Metastasio—are in the tradition of *opera buffa*; but in characterization and pointedness of comment they emerge as far greater than the conventions of that tradition might have been thought to allow. *La clemenza di Tito*, composed in 1791 for the coronation of Leopold II as King of Bohemia, is *opera seria*. *Die Zauberflöte* ("The Magic Flute") of the same year is a German opera based on dramatic ideas popular in Vienna and incorporated into the libretto by Emanuel Schikaneder and on the current Viennese love of rich and colourful orchestration. *The Magic Flute* is in part a fairy story, but it deals with the occult and embraces aspects of Freemasonry (Mozart and Schikaneder were both Masons); above all, it has passion and emotion. "Into the overture," writes Albert Einstein, "which is anything but a *Singspiel* overture, [Mozart] compressed the struggle and victory of mankind, using the symbolic means of polyphony: working out, laborious working out in the development section; struggle and triumph."

Thus Professor Einstein discovers in Mozart the approach of the nineteenth-century musical attitude. That this should be so was inevitable, for Mozart was a child of his age, and each age carries the seed of the next. But Mozart was also the end of an epoch. In manner he summarized the reasonableness of the Age of Enlightenment, the clarity and grace of the symphonic ideal. "In art", wrote Bernard Shaw at the time of the Mozart centenary of 1891, "the highest success is to be the last of your race, not the first. Anybody, almost, can make a beginning: the difficulty is to make an end—to do what cannot be bettered."

9

Revolution

FROM the early Middle Ages until the end of the eighteenth century Western music may seem to have mirrored social changes, and religious and political divisions; it cannot, however, be said that many composers set out with the deliberate intention of composing works that should exert moral influence in their own right. But in the nineteenth century numerous composers did— directly involved in the major issues of the period, and inspired by the greater general impact made by music on society and by the expanding resources of music itself.

The French Revolution took place towards the end of the lives of Mozart and Haydn, but during Beethoven's young and impressionable years. The effects of the French Revolution were felt in every department of life and thought, and what is called Romantic music may well— in its first phase—be studied in relation to the feelings and the events which changed the face of Europe so drastically. In spite of wars, and rumours of wars, and of provocative and forward-looking literature, the eighteenth century was an era of at least relative repose and tranquillity; things were generally assumed to be as they were because it had been so ordained. The nineteenth century, on the other hand, was an age of unrest: after the French Revolution came the Napoleonic Wars, in mid-century the working-class revolt of 1848, and for the rest a continual state of turmoil as groups of people, and nations, attempted—often through recourse to arms—to achieve independence.

Of the great composers of the Romantic epoch, Beethoven was affected by the revolutionary principles that came from France; Schumann, and, to a larger extent, Wagner, were implicated in the 1848 Revolution; while Weber, Chopin, Liszt, and Verdi showed strong nationalist sympathies. Dissatisfaction with the immediate past and the development of a new style of musical expression —which engaged the attention of every major composer in one way or another—was the chief mark of the great French composer Hector Berlioz.

The idea that music might exercise moral influence, strongly held during the Romantic era, derived in part from the personal background of many composers. Beethoven followed old custom. He was the son of a musician of the Rhineland court of Bonn, and was almost automatically apprenticed to his father's craft. Schubert's antecedents were musical, he lived in a powerful musical environment, and his dereliction from schoolmaster to composer was not really surprising. With such composers as Berlioz, Schumann, Mendelssohn, and Wagner, however, the case was different, for they were all endowed with the privileges of an all-round education. They were of the independent middle class, trained in liberal and scientific studies at university level. Each, therefore, brought to music a wealth of experience that had not often characterized earlier musicians, who lived in times when a creative musician was regarded merely as a craftsman, required to produce works to order.

In the nineteenth century we find music invading (or being invaded by) painting, poetry, history, biography, philosophy, politics; seeking specifically to express the "spirit" of the individual composer, of his nation, of mankind in general; and thus to assume the quality and purpose of a language. In the nineteenth century the composer (although not infrequently left to starve) became a figure of public importance and contention. Because the idea of the hero, or the superman, came to be promoted, especially by the German philosophers, the notable composer, whether dead or alive, was eventually regarded as heroic, in a special way. Thus statues were erected in large numbers to the memory of deceased composers—especially in Germany; and biographical writing on musical subjects became a steady industry.

Music, helped by the printing of cheap editions, became a universal art, supported by crowned heads on the one hand but also by large numbers of choral singers who occupied a more modest place in society. The middle classes, imitating the habits of their social superiors, sought often to parade their respectability by purchasing pianos, by insisting on music lessons for their children, and by encouraging the domestic cult of instrumental and vocal ensemble. Music was so much up-graded in the nineteenth century that Walter Pater, in his study *The Renaissance*, could declare that: "All art constantly aspires towards the condition of music."

In short, music became popular, in the widest meaning of this misused word; as popular as drama in the time of Shakespeare, and of painting in the age of Rembrandt. It was also, of necessity, for the first time predominantly secular in inspiration.

The secularity of music laid stress on certain aspects of art congenial to the post-Rousseau artist-philosopher: art became its own law-giver, being no longer subject to the ruling of a higher authority (this ideal was fully worked out by Shelley in his *Defence of Poetry*): it developed in

The Concert Party, after a picture attributed to Giorgione. Art aspiring to the condition of music

virtuosity, which element was also responsible, in part at least, for a wider popular appeal; and, finally, the impact of art—and more especially music, which holds the greatest power in this respect—on the senses was more fully realized.

It is not perhaps unfair to observe that the first impact made by Beethoven was on the senses of his Viennese audiences; he was, in fact, a sensational composer—the word carrying halfway from its simpler root-meaning to our present interpretation of its meaning.

Beethoven was in his early twenties when he moved from the provincial backwater of Bonn to the musical metropolis of Vienna, where, an unruly but not ungrateful pupil, he had lessons from Johann Albrechtsberger, the great theorist, and Josef Haydn. It was as pianist that he first won recognition. "It was acknowledged", wrote an anonymous Englishman of Beethoven's day in *The Harmonicon* of 1823:

> that he had studied the piano-forte with a success that enabled him to excel all the masters of his time; that there was a spirit, a fire, and brilliancy of execution, which no one could equal; and that nothing was wanting to perfect his performance, but a certain precision and distinction of touch. It was unanimously agreed, that his triumph was in the execution of a fantasia, and in the art of varying any given theme without the least premeditation. In such extempore performance, his power was inimitable: he was considered to approach the nearest to Mozart, as he is allowed never since to have had a rival except in the brilliant Himmel.

Himmel was a Berlin musician, famous in his own day but soon forgotten. Beethoven once met him, and, regarding his talents as overpraised, treated him with a characteristic absence of flattery. Beethoven's honesty of outlook often provoked difficult social situations and his own reputation for unmannerliness.

Beethoven's feeling for the pianoforte, assisted by the development of the instrument in power and tonal resource and by its new absolute supremacy in the field of the keyboard, is fully expressed in his monumental series of 32 sonatas and five concertos. To us they appear to begin where Haydn left off (in 1796 the three sonatas of *Opus 2* were dedicated to Haydn). This is because the form used by Beethoven—as also in his symphonies—is that common to all classical-period composers. The music-lovers of the Romantic era, however, were impressed more by content than by form, a matter in which, perhaps, we may learn from them, and their first reactions were summarized in the *Allgemeine Musikalische Zeitung*. Beethoven's music showed "harshness of modulation, melodies more singular than pleasing, and a constant struggle to be original".

The "constant struggle to be original" is equally apparent in each one of the nine symphonies. The factors that proclaim originality are: the strong, vital, percussive rhythms that dominate every movement; the urgency of the dynamics which are so disposed as to effect startling disturbances in expectation; the wide range of instrumental colouring extracted from the same orchestral forces used by Beethoven's less surprising contemporaries; the new relationships engineered between tonal centres; the quality and apparent simplicity of melodic outline; the wide range of *tempi* employed; and a general mastery of form, which made the outlines of sonata style guiding principles rather than essential obligations.

Beethoven's handling of musical design and expression is some sort of index to part of his own character. It may reasonably be argued that this applies to all musicians, indeed to anybody who moulds any substance, or ideas, according to some intention; but Beethoven held views on the function of music in society. To his friend, pupil, and patron, the Archduke Rudolph, he once expressed himself thus: "Liberty and progress are the goals of art just as of life in general. If we are not as solid as the old masters, the refinement of civilization has at least enlarged our outlook."

The enlarged outlook is indicated by the circumstances which led to the composition of the "Eroica" symphony in the years 1803–4, of the "Pastoral" symphony four or five years later, of the "Choral" symphony, with its last gigantic movement based on Schiller's *Ode to Joy* in the years 1822–23, of the "heroic" opera *Fidelio*, and the

Beethoven, from an old print

overtures *Coriolanus*, *Egmont*, and the music for the *Prometheus* ballet.

In such works—and by implication in his more abstract chamber music and concertos—Beethoven attempts to state a point of view: the point of view of the Romantic artist, striving to associate himself with the forward march of social philosophies. Some admired, and still admire, Beethoven for this reason. Others, however, esteem him because his music is supreme as music, by musical standards, in the sphere of music alone.

So it was in his own day. His livelihood depended to a considerable extent on the generosity of wealthy and aristocratic patrons, whose love for music and frequent skill in the art was an enduring feature of Viennese life. Such men as the Archduke Rudolph, the Princes Lichnovsky and Lobkovitz, the Counts Rasumovsky and von Waldstein—the list of patrons is a long one and is immortalized in Beethoven's dedications—represented a traditional way of life. Revolution, by which they were surrounded, was no part of their interpretation of art; but through experience and opportunity they had high standards in musical judgement. Therefore, to their honour, they did what they could to support an evident genius, however explosive his personality and uncongenial his opinions and manners.

Less enlightened amateurs of music, as well as the "academic" musicians and critics who profited by conservative habits of thought, found Beethoven's music perplexing. When the overture *The Consecration of the House* was first played at a Philharmonic concert in London the critics were cautious and said exactly what a critic of today might say of a new work: "This overture is one of those compositions which, to understand thoroughly, requires more than a single hearing, and we hope to have an opportunity of entering further into its merits."

In this way, too, a reviewer of 1823 disposed of the now famous set of "Diabelli" Variations (Opus 120): "Beethoven's latest work . . . is, we fear, confirmatory of the report . . . of this great composer having, from deafness, lost some of that discriminating judgement, which he possessed in so striking a degree before his sense of hearing was impaired. We pass over several unaccountable singularities in this work, and can only allow ourselves to observe, generally, that while it manifests either an entire loss of that sense so needful to a musician, or a degree of neglect in the engraver, unparalleled and incredible, it shows that the author has not yet quite exhausted the fund of ideas, exclusively his own—upon which, for the benefit of mankind, he has been drawing nearly thirty years."

Beethoven was the great musician of Vienna in the first quarter of the nineteenth century. There were other composers, however, who were greatly esteemed—usually because they were less provoking, more successful in a worldly sense, and, no doubt, much happier as individuals: Eybler, Seyfried, Czerny, Diabelli, Weigl, and so on. Ignez Seyfried, who wrote music for Beethoven's funeral, was a much-sought-after teacher. Of his pupils one achieved immortality: Johann Strauss, whose prolificacy (and also of course that of his son) in composing waltzes really commenced the more general idea still prevalent of the true nature of "popular" music. It is easiest, perhaps, to hit the mark by suggesting that the Strausses, catching the feverish mood of post-war society in the nineteenth century, extracted the "pop" element from "popular", and found it profitable to develop.

The history of great art is frequently the record of unsuccessful men. Among these was Franz Schubert, who lived inconspicuously and uncomfortably in another part of Vienna when Beethoven was resident there. Schubert had none of Beethoven's grand ideas. He wrote music because he could do nothing else so effectively. He was modest of his talents, and on his death-bed was planning to take further lessons. His genius was of the lyrical order, Beethoven's of the epical; yet, as it happened, the time was ripe for just such genius as that of Schubert, for there was to hand a new and immense supply of lyrical poetry.

The Romantic revival in poetry (in an age in which poetry was widely read and discussed) diffused many ideas. Folk-art and folk-poetry—and, a little more distantly, perhaps, the folk who made the art and the poetry—were fashionable; nature was extolled, as also the "spirits" of nature; the enchantment of distant places was advertised; human passions were given a freer rein; and the whole tendency was away from the rational towards the imaginative. English poetry and the Scottish verses of Burns were vastly influential, and Shakespeare enjoyed a revival of fame as a precursor of Romantic sentiment. German writers, inspired by the general atmosphere of Romanticism which was congenial to the German mystical temperament, fell over themselves in an enthusiasm to supply lyrical poetry, but they were also inspired by a deep love of Germany, and by a laudable desire to disprove the former widely held theory that German was not a "literary" language.

The romantic poets of Germany, after Goethe and Schiller, included Hölderlin, Novalis, Brentano, Chamisso, Kerner, Uhland, von Eichendorff, Rückert, Müller, von Platen, Heine, Mörike, Hebbel, and Geibel. Examples of their work form the greater part of the *Oxford Book of German Verse* and represent the stimulus afforded to so many musicians of the new era. This body of poetry, characterized as a whole by a musical sensibility —in the selection and arrangement of words—that often outstrips sense and overcomes a frequent monotony of subject-matter, calls for a musical setting in a way in which the more self-contained and "literary" verses of the greater English romantics do not. It is not surprising, therefore, that the opportunity offered was seized by a large number of composers, of whom Schubert, Franz, Schumann, Mendelssohn, Brahms, and Wolf are the most notable.

The finest settings of these composers have one singularly powerful quality. They cancel the sentimentality that lies in the words by a precision, craftsmanship, and understanding of the general idea of the poetry that is peculiar to music.

The German *Lied* is a union of separate functions, as represented by words, vocal melody—which arises out of the words, and pianoforte accompaniment—which translates the overtones of verbal meaning; and undoubtedly the greatest, most spontaneous and lyrical of these composers was Schubert, whose 600 songs brought into the drawing-rooms of select households—in the first place in Vienna—the impulses of the age reduced to terms apt for domestic understanding. This would not have been possible had the new, evocative tones of the pianoforte not been available.

It is no disparagement of Schubert to emphasize his lyrical genius: some, as Beethoven, are born to be creators in the epic mould; others are predestined to express equally large truths in smaller compass. It is the complement to the heroic aspirations and achievements of Beethoven. And even—as in the "Unfinished" and "Great C Major" symphonies, and in the chamber music—when Schubert follows the more public patterns of musical design he does not depart from the lyrical principles, which endow his major works with charm, tenderness, and ebullience.

More consciously than Schubert, Schumann, whose approach to music was by way of literature and philosophy, endeavoured to express in music the deepest personal feelings, and to this end he experimented with the vocabulary of music in order to make that art more definitive in terms of language. The most immediately expressive of Schumann's works are his songs (the accompaniments are often extremely original and significant) and his collections of pianoforte pieces, of which the greater part are characterized by evocative titles, and lie in such collections as *Papillons*, *Carnaval*, *Kinderszenen* (Schumann was a great master of the small piece ideal for both the fingers and the quick-moving imagination of the child), *Phantasiestücke*, *Waldszenen*, and so on. Into the larger forms of concerto—especially that for pianoforte in A minor—and symphony Schumann carried his original attitude with varying degrees of success. But unifying all his music, and uniting with that of his great compatriot contemporaries, was an abiding sense that German music mattered because it was German. Thus we discover a new factor: that of nationalism.

Temperament and aptitude being what they are, composers often found themselves between two fires. One such was Felix Mendelssohn, whose powerful and quick intellect, as well as the influence of his gifted family, led him naturally to logical modes of thought and expression. His music, and particularly his symphonic and chamber music, has clarity of purpose and design deriving from his avowed love and regard for the greatest exemplar of classicism—Mozart. But the spirit of the age opened doors to a new world, which Mendelssohn recognized as possessing its own values. Therefore he imbued his art with colour (he was a brilliant orchestrator with an aptitude for decorating his scores with enchanting washes of subtly bright tints of woodwind and high string tone) and with visual ideas. Thus we have the originality of such works as the *Hebrides*, *Melusina*, and *Calm Sea and Prosperous Voyage* overtures, the Violin concerto, and the *Italian* and *Scottish* symphonies.

Mendelssohn was a fine player, both pianist and organist; an administrator whose powers of organization benefited the cities of Düsseldorf, Leipzig, Berlin; an orchestral director with authority and broad sympathies; and a scholar. Like Schumann, whose friend he was, Mendelssohn was passionately concerned to revive the older glories of German music. Between them Schumann and Mendelssohn rescued Schubert's "Great C major" symphony from obscurity long after its composer's death, and saw that it was performed; revived the fame of Johann Sebastian Bach; and assisted in the rehabilitation, in Germany at any rate, of George Frideric Handel. In so far as he was the principal architect of the great teaching school of Germany, the Conservatorium in Leipzig, to which students from many lands came in the second half of the nineteenth century, Mendelssohn exerted a strong influence on musical style that was not always advantageous. Many musicians, in fact, were content to submerge too much of their own individuality and the needs of their own communities in an idiom that, through a succession of theorists and composition teachers who were dogmatic in respect of the "rules" of art rather than its principles, became merely artificial.

In the last paragraph a word appeared which deserves closer scrutiny: "individuality"—with which may be equated "personality". The music of Beethoven, of Schubert, of Schumann, of Mendelssohn (such a group of German names is sufficient to demonstrate why Germany became so powerful in music at that period) is distinctive.

With some experience one may readily recognize the one
from the other. It is much less easy to do this in respect of
eighteenth-century music. Even though these few composers wrote the same kind of music—each, for instance,
composed symphonies, sonatas, and chamber music with
one eye on the classical form and tradition—they adopted
different attitudes, and thus developed a more or less expressive manner of writing which gives many hints to the
composer's personality. Beethoven's music is dramatic;
Schubert's lyrical; Schumann's dreamlike; Mendelssohn's
orderly, precise, and carefully coloured. Each composer,
moreover, had an eye on an audience which he was,
sometimes consciously but often unconsciously, trying to
persuade to his point of view.

Music which is thus persuasive is also revolutionary, in
that it proclaims the virtues of new ideas. If it is not too
paradoxical revolutions in music may be silent; that is, the
composer, anxious to promulgate new ideas, may take old
bottles, fill them with new wine, and leave the public to
decide for themselves the quality of the contents of the
bottle. Despite the protestations of some critics all the
composers hitherto mentioned were general believers in
this principle. When, however, we move to France we find
a radical difference.

Hector Berlioz was a few years younger than Schubert
and a few years older than Schumann and Mendelssohn,
both of whom were much impressed by his personality and
startled and even captivated by his music. Berlioz was a
Parisian, the son of a doctor, whose profession he was intended to follow. He was born in 1803, in which year war
broke out again between France and England. In both
countries patriotism was aflame. The French, inspired in
the first place by the ideas of the Revolution, were also
conscious of the new sense of "glory" promised by

Napoleon, now on his way from being First Consul to becoming Emperor (which act, in 1804, caused Beethoven to destroy the dedication of his "Eroica" symphony). Artists in France, always near the centre of thought since the spacious days of patronage of Louis XIV, leapt at opportunity. A particular type of French romanticism was born, with strong literary bias, and such writers as Victor Hugo, Théophile Gautier, Alexandre Dumas, and Honoré Balzac, and the painters Jean Louis Géricault and Ferdinand Delacroix flourished. They overthrew the classical traditions of literature and art, imbuing both with new life and colour, seeking inspiration from "real life" on the one hand and from the romantically interpreted writings of Dante, Shakespeare, Scott, and Byron on the other. Berlioz, distinguished as a music-student at the Paris Conservatoire by his dissatisfaction at the conventional teaching and by (to his tutors) his odd compositions, endeavoured to bring similar ideas into music.

The most striking feature of Berlioz's music is its colour. His mode of composition led him to regard orchestration as a department of music equal to form, melody, harmony, counterpoint, and so on; just as painters made paint important, so did he in a special sense teach that music is a matter of sound. The range of Berlioz's skill in orchestration may be appreciated in his autobiographical *Fantastic* symphony, in the viola concerto (the first of its kind) *Harold in Italy*, in the great *Messe des Morts* composed in memory of the soldiers killed in the conquest of Algeria in 1837, in the operas *Les Troyens* and *Benvenuto Cellini*, in the oratorio *L'Enfance du Christ*, and in a number of concert overtures and other works. There is also a book on instrumentation, which was translated into English by Mary Cowden Clarke, to introduce the keen student to Berlioz's attitude towards music. In this work there is an unmistakable and self-evident romantic impulse, giving to it a special place among musical treatises, which as a class are hardly distinguished by warmth of feeling or enthusiasm. Enthusiasm is another word particularly applicable to Romantic art in all its phases.

Berlioz was an excellent writer of prose, and his essays and autobiographical writings are an important part of his output. They help to elucidate his music, as this was so strongly marked by literary and by narrative impulse. Berlioz was not the originator of programme music (the term applies, rather loosely, to all descriptive music and anything in a score vaguely resembling a bird-call or other "natural" sound will produce vigorous footnotes entailing the use of the word "programme music"), but he was, perhaps, the first really to make music with a programme. The *Fantastic* symphony bound together by one theme—the *idée fixe*, which represents a particular person—is a story, and the listener is supposed to derive much information about Berlioz, his dreams, his love-life, and so on, from the combination of literary narrative (provided by Berlioz for the first performance) and highly picturesque music. Whether the listener does, in fact, learn as much of what he was expected by the composer to learn is quite another matter.

However, many people have persuaded themselves that music can "tell a story", and Berlioz, basing much of his music on the works of Shakespeare, Scott, Moore, Byron, and Goethe, has contributed much to a theory fairly consistently held by concert-goers. Moreover, his influence on musicians was profound. Some, especially the rising nationalists of Russia, were thrilled by his technique and by his revolutionary ardour; others by his principles of musical vocabulary and structure.

The public orchestral concert is a relatively new feature

The old Gewandhaus, Leipzig

in the history of music. Such concerts were given in the eighteenth century, especially in Leipzig, Vienna, Paris, and London, but it was not until the nineteenth century that they began to exercise wide appeal and general influence. Composers looked more and more to the orchestra to convey their musical ideas; the middle classes took over the previous privileges and prerogatives of the aristocracy; instrument-makers made instruments more efficient, more refined, and more powerful. One thing bound up with the other, and in the end architects were called upon to provide suitable halls for the housing of such concerts. Part of the achievement of the Romantic composers, therefore, was to inaugurate an era in which people listened to rather than performed music. But that, in the music-conscious atmosphere of the mid-nineteenth century, was still some way off.

We return to Beethoven, Schubert, Schumann, and Mendelssohn. Each composed music for the pianoforte which is still part of the amateur pianist's repertoire.

Between them they gave to the instrument that formed part of every self-respecting household a century ago a character and personality of its own. Pianoforte music, especially in the miniatures of Schumann and Mendelssohn, was distinctively pianoforte music; a special branch of music. When anything is denoted as special it implies a specialist, and part of the Romantic movement was the beginning of the reign of the musical specialist.

Pre-Romantic composers wrote all kinds of music, as required, and without exception they were competent performers themselves. Schumann had once hoped to be a pianist, but an accident to a finger, caused by trying to take a mechanical short-cut to virtuoso excellence, prevented the realization of his hopes. His pianoforte music was made famous by another person—a famous pianist; in this case it was his wife, Clara, who was the founder of a large school of solo pianists. Berlioz was not a performer, but as a conductor he helped to establish the later dominance of the professional conductor whose speciality was conducting.

The unspoken aim of every new departure was self-expression. The composer, the conductor, the singer, the pianist all aimed at this desirable end. Except for the composer all had to do it vicariously, that is by using the art of another: the same obtained in the theatre, where the actor was also becoming more aware of his separate and individual importance. It may be said that all this is latent in art, and that is a large part of its purpose. But the separation of creator and performer brought its own hazards. The singer or the player became increasingly esteemed for his technical skill or for his showmanship: people went to see performers like Liszt and Paganini as well as to hear them. It does not need pointing out that the self-expression so much cultivated by the Romantics is very much alive at the present time, and not always in the most satisfactory or satisfying manner.

But there was another form of expression: that of *national* aspirations. One of the most characteristically romantic of composers was Frédéric Chopin, half-French and half-Pole, whose career was marked by his devotion to the ideal of Polish nationhood. The titles of many of his works—*Polonaises* and *Mazurkas*—are an index in themselves to this devotion, and in such pieces he consciously emphasized his faith by utilizing the rhythms and tune patterns of folk-music. Chopin was a poetic composer, who understood in a particular way the poetical quality of the pianoforte. By exploiting this quality he produced a new style of music, which to this day stands apart from other music by its high beauty and originality. The *Waltzes* (a refinement of the all-conquering popular dance of the nineteenth century), *Préludes*, *Nocturnes*, *Études*, *Ballades*, as well as the *Polonaises* and *Mazurkas*, are essentially and inviolably for the pianoforte and no other medium. They represent almost every facet of Romantic sensibility, but one can never forget that Chopin was a Pole. His last engagement in the winter of 1848 was at a concert in aid of Polish refugees held at the Guildhall in London.

Similarly one does not forget that Liszt—whose biography again is thoroughly "romantic" from beginning to end—was a Hungarian, whose native country music echoes in the *Rhapsodies*. Liszt was a man of many parts. As a pianist his prodigious technique may be re-created from a glance at almost any one of his 1,300 compositions (of which many were transcriptions). As a composer he carried a stage further the *idée fixe* of Berlioz, often basing his works on "representative themes" which bound together large-scale works by their recurrence in different guises; he experimented with new and then strange harmonic progressions; he instituted the Symphonic Poem—another consequence of programme music. He was influential and always progressive. He was also generous and of great help to other composers whom he regarded as hopes of the future. Among those indebted in one way or another to Liszt were Brahms, Grieg (a Norwegian), MacDowell (an American), and Richard Wagner.

With Wagner we come back to opera, and the changes in this art form will act as a summary to this chapter, for opera is, as it were, the shop-window of music—and particularly where Romanticism is in the air.

It becomes almost monotonous to stress the particular place occupied in the story of opera by Italian artists, but the vitality of the Italians in this province is an abiding, and invaluable, element in music. The Italians invented opera, and they popularized opera—so much so in their own country that an opera audience there was, and is, moved by the same mixture of passion and critical perception that the British reserve for football matches. Thus they have preserved some of the fundamentals of music—its nearness to the simplest emotions, its basic impulse from the voice; its power to astonish and to persuade by familiar and often obvious means—and in so doing have frequently given to opera the status of folk-art. Popular devotion to this art since the seventeenth century was responsible for great singers—who, although naturally endowed as seems to be the case with almost every Italian, were tutored with rigour—and, at length, great instrumentalists, wonderful opera houses, talented librettists, and composers of all sorts—bad, indifferent, good and supreme. The plain truth is that there was opportunity, without which no artist can thrive.

Opera seria and *opera buffa* were the two main channels

for expression in the eighteenth century and the conventions died hard, for the Italian public knew quite well what it liked and stuck to what was established. Outside Italy, especially in Germany and Austria, Italian music, as we have seen, came under fire, partly for æsthetic and partly for political reasons. But change was irresistible; no self-respecting composer ever ignores what is happening to music through technical change and will ever incline to enlarging his own powers of statement and expression. Those who don't are usually those who can't.

One of the great influences in Italian music, whether sacred or secular, in the period under consideration, was Niccoló Zingarelli, whose operas were as famous in Paris as in Milan, and whose gifts as director won him the coveted appointments at Milan Cathedral and the Sistine Chapel in Rome. Zingarelli was a brilliant musician and a great teacher; among his pupils were Bellini and Donizetti. He was also a great patriot, and an account of his relations with the Emperor Napoleon is some indication of the proud position then occupied by opera composers who were Italian.

Napoleon, a great lover of music, had heard operas by Zingarelli in Paris, in Loreto, in Vienna. In 1811 he proclaimed his son King of Rome and commanded a solemn *Te Deum* to be sung in St. Peter's. The civil and ecclesiastical authorities made all preparations and a large company was assembled for the occasion. But it could not take place. Zingarelli staged a one-man strike, refusing to acknowledge any foreign domination of his country. Napoleon ordered the composer's arrest and removal to Paris—where he was liberated and presented with a pension. Thus both parties came out of the affair with credit.

Already in Paris was another famous Italian, Cherubini,

who had conducted the Italian opera in that city and was shortly to become head of the Conservatoire. Cherubini rejected the conventions of Italian popular style, followed the examples of Gluck and Mozart, and imbued his own operas with a degree of seriousness and unconventionality that was at first not to the liking of the pleasure-loving Parisians. In such works as *Lodoïska* and *Médée* there was evident a strong desire to accommodate the music to the sentiments of the libretti.

Bellini, whose melodic idiom inspired his friend Chopin, and Donizetti managed to catch the tide of Romanticism in a less revolutionary manner. Cherubini explored orchestral colours more intently. Bellini and Donizetti eliminated the worst excesses from vocal style, and chose subjects of more up-to-date appeal for their operas. Bellini was affected by French literature and his libretti were often based on French originals, the most popular source being the dramas of Augustin Scribe. Donizetti, whose comic operas—of which *Don Pasquale* is the principal—essayed the most typically Romantic plots and looked for suitable colour and mystery in the works of Scott (*Lucia di Lammermoor*), Byron (*Marino Faliero*), and Hugo (*Lucrezia Borgia*). In Rossini, a world figure and almost a legend in his lifetime, we meet another Italian whose success in Paris was enormous. Although he was a great master of *opera buffa*—of which the most splendid example is *The Barber of Seville*—Rossini caught up with the age in which he lived by composing the "grand opera" *William Tell*, after the play by Schiller. *William Tell* is "grand" both musically and spectacularly (a subject with a Swiss setting almost inevitably implies grandeur, for the Alps—so much visited by Romantic poets—are at once in mind), and thoroughly characteristic of another aspect of the Romantic art,

Covent Garden, 1810, from an old print

The great exponent of grand opera, however, was Giacomo Meyerbeer, a German-Jew of great gifts and a remarkable feeling for the spectacular. His notable works, which again won great renown in Paris where the composer lived, were *Robert le Diable, Les Huguenots* (religious subjects and references were conspicuous in nineteenth-century opera) and *L'Africaine*. In all of them Meyerbeer endeavoured to match the stage spectacle by magnificent vocal parts and striking orchestral effects, which necessitated the employment of new instruments, or old instruments in new ways. Among composers influenced by Meyerbeer the most conspicuous was Richard Wagner.

But Wagner drew also on more consciously German models. The Italian composers here noticed came to terms with their own tradition and with the spirit of the age in their own, often opportunist, way. In Germany, on the other hand, composers as often as not set themselves the task of displacing Italian opera, and of creating a national style that grew from native origins. The spirit of the old *Singspiel*, which was a popular non-aristocratic art, lived on; it was honoured by backward-glancing musicians because it preserved the German language in some sort of secular and common musical context.

After Mozart the next great name in German opera was that of Carl Maria von Weber, a relative of Mozart's wife, whose brief career makes a notable chapter in German operatic history. Weber, in *Der Freischütz*, *Euryanthe*, *Preciosa*, and *Oberon*, introduced legend, symbolism, magic, mystery, and a zest for faraway sights and sounds into music, thus complementing the work of the major writers and dramatists of his time. Like Rossini and Meyerbeer, Weber was a vivid orchestrator, but with a deeper sense of what might be termed the inner character of the instruments of the orchestra. Weber's music—even in the brilliant *Invitation to the Dance*—does not give the impression of superficiality, because, in contrast to the other composers mentioned, there is greater activity in the elements of melody and harmony than in the more immediately successful music of his less idealistic contemporaries.

Weber explored all the colourful facets of Romanticism. Heinrich Marschner, sometime Weber's assistant at the Dresden Opera, was drawn to the melodramatic, and his best-known opera was *Der Vampyr*, the horrific story having been prepared by Marschner's brother-in-law Wilhelm Wohlbrück from Byronic and other sources. Marschner also attracted Wagner. He was admired too by Schumann, and the incorporation of a theme from Marschner's opera *Der Templer* into the finale of Schumann's *Études*

Symphoniques is another example of the nearness of narrative to music at that time. Schumann's work was dedicated to the English composer Sterndale Bennett. Marschner's opera was on a libretto derived from Scott's *Ivanhoe*. How better pay a compliment to an English composer than by referring obliquely to a Scottish writer through another German composer?

German comic opera found its best exponent in Gustav Lortzing, a singer in the opera house in Leipzig. His *Czar und Zimmermann*, clearly drawn from the pattern of *Singspiel*, enjoyed enormous success in Leipzig—in which city German cultural independence was highly prized—and was one of the earliest German operas to reach the New World, having its American première in New York in 1857.

It is a relief, sometimes, to turn to the charm and affectionate intimacy of Lortzing. Such works as *Der Waffenschmied*, which still appeals to a provincial German audience as do the operas of Gilbert and Sullivan to the English, bring the spirit of the Romantic revolution to a domestic plane, and remind us that at the heart of the Romantic Movement was an intention to make the arts, and learning, available to all. This is the natural consequence of the cult of the individual. How it is to be achieved is still a lively problem; but Romanticism asks rather than answers questions.

10

Full Tide

Aᴛᴛᴇʀ a successful revolution comes a period of consolidation, or, perhaps more accurately, a period of
apparent consolidation—for in human affairs nothing is
ever absolutely stable. In that lies the adventure of living,
and in this instance the adventure of listening. W. B.
Yeats devotes a large part of his famous Introduction to
the *Oxford Book of Modern Verse* to this condition; his nodal
word is "flux", which is simply interpreted in the phrase:
"we tumble out of one pickle into another"

By the middle of the nineteenth century the first impulse
of revolutionary Romanticism was all but spent, and its
principles had begun to harden into conventions. Nature
poetry, with its own distinctive form of metre and language,
had acquired something of the artifice that the pioneer
poets in this genre had sought to displace; drama had also
suffered a like remove. Music, trailing behind literature,
had changed its status. It was for the most part repre-
sentational, often trying to describe what in terms of music
is indescribable. Every self-respecting composer learned
how to define nature, history, philosophy, and even issues
of a political nature, in a "musical diction" that was, and
is, it must be confessed, often impressive and sometimes
nearly convincing.

Thus we accept readily that the pianoforte works of
Edward MacDowell are "about" America, the orchestral

works of Smetana, Dvořák, Fibich, Janáček, and Suk "about" Bohemia; the cantatas, overtures, and symphonies of Gade, Svendsen, and Nielsen "about" Denmark; the songs of Parry, even more the variations, marches, symphonies and oratorios of Elgar, "about" England; the songs and rhapsodies of Stanford "about" Ireland; the tone poems of Sibelius "about" Finland; the minor works of Nordraak and Grieg "about" Norway; the operas, symphonies, overtures, and ballets of a school of Russian composers stretching from Lvov and Glinka to the early works of Stravinsky as "about" Russia. The conviction that music can tell a coherent story in a manner not dissimilar from literary modes of expression still persists—even though the vocabulary of music is different, and romantic attitudes are still cultivated; especially in communities strongly aware of patriotism in its old and, maybe, its natural form. The music of Copland is "about" America; that of Shostakovich and Kabalevsky "about" Russia.

The reason for this lies partly inside the province of art, and partly outside.

Music appeals to the senses, and thereon it makes its first impressions. For reasons of which we are not fully aware, as stated in the first chapter of this book, a sound, a sequence of sounds, or a combination of sounds can move us to sorrow or gladness. But there must be a variety in such stimulation, for the imaginative system, like the physical system, can after a time become impervious. We enjoy the waltz, for instance, but we enjoy it differently from the generation to whom it was a new phenomenon.

In the course of time music developed a vocabulary of its own. The rhythmic pattern of a *pavan* (because the *pavan* was a stately dance in the first place) denoted stateliness; that of a jig (or *gigue*) liveliness. The shape of a

Russian folk-dancers, from a porcelain figure

trepak, as shown in Tchaikovsky's *Nutcracker Suite*, suggests a wild animation, because that is what we have conditioned ourselves to consider the proper quality of the unfamiliar behaviour of Cossack peasantry. Major tonality is different from minor tonality. Because composers for a long time used the one in conjunction with words of a generally optimistic character and the other to opposite texts it is assumed that major spells cheerfulness and minor, misery. Upper notes and harmonies denote brightness; lower notes, darkness; discords, doubt and/or conflict. Needless to say the tonal characteristics of instruments also suggest definitions. The glockenspiel denotes gaiety in the carefree Apprentices' Dance in Act III of Wagner's *Meistersinger*; the horn solos in Brahms's first two symphonies are evocative of warmth and geniality; the saxophone in Vaughan Williams's *Job* is sinister and insinuating; the bassoon as used by Richard Strauss or Elgar portrays oddity or senility. The diligent student may continue to compile a log-book of such equations.

The total list of references by music to the world outside is very long and very impressive. But in nine cases out of ten we believe in the narrative virtue of music because it has previously been explained to us what we should interpret. Programme music—that is almost the whole of music composed under the Romantic influence—requires a programme.

Programme music was urged on its way by the laudable doctrine that music should be in touch with common life. This was the guiding principle of Beethoven, also of Berlioz, and of Schumann. Too often, however, the enchantment of art for art's sake proved too strong. Sterndale Bennett wrote an overture entitled *The Naiads*. It was once highly praised. Romantic make-believe accepted it at Schumann's valuation:

"While listening to the overture", he wrote,

it needs but little fancy in any hearer to imagine that he sees lovely interlaced groups of sporting, bathing Naiads, while the soft flutes and oboes suggest surrounding rose bushes, haunted by cooing turtle-doves; even prosaic brains may be certain of experiencing at least such an impression as that awakened by Goethe in his *Fisherman*, that is to say, the summer feelings that may be softly cooled by flowing waters —so glassy clear, so agreeably and invitingly the music extends itself before us. . . .

The reaction of one group of children of today to this, summarized in one expressive morsel of current idiomati nursery English, is probably not untypical: "soppy". Bu. this was the direction followed by much nineteenth- and early twentieth-century music.

Descriptive composers used new chords and new chordal progressions. The harmonic language of music, therefore, became more complex and varied. The chordal vocabularies of Wagner, Strauss, and Mahler are full of most vivid idioms, whose conjunction led to new and unexpected modes of progression. The classical tonal scheme was basically simple and clear-cut (even though Mozart, Haydn, and Beethoven frequently turned away from rule and followed intuition), involving a rigorous system that had been defined by Rameau and other theorists. The masters of the late nineteenth century, logical according to their own calculations, added to the existing system, so that by the time Wagner composed *Tristan and Isolde* in 1865 it was clear that the classical formulas had had their day. At least, it was clear that no further progress could be made in extending the harmonic processes along the accustomed lines, and that separate and self-contained "keys" were a hindrance rather than a help.

In searching for additional powers of self-expression the Romantics radically affected the material of music. What was true of harmony (the most effective of the means at the Romantic composer's disposal) was also true of melody, now modified by a general and enthusiastic pursuit of folk-idiom and rhythm. It was even more true of the instruments of the orchestra. Xylophone, glockenspiel, saxophone, celesta, tuba . . .; many new instruments took their place in the orchestra of the nineteenth century, and the old ones learned to play new tricks. There are few Romantic works which do not exemplify this, but a particularly impressive score which allies a zest for tonal exploration with a desire to illustrate is Sibelius's *Luonnotar* (for soprano solo and orchestra). The story is of the birth of a Finnish legendary hero, from the marriage of the winds and the waves with Luonnotar, the Spirit of the Air.

"It is", writes Cecil Gray,

> one of the most remarkable scores of modern times, abounding in curious and interesting experiments in sonority. A particular noteworthy feature is the writing for the kettle drums, six in number and requiring two players, which are continually playing in minor seconds simultaneously. Striking, too, is the writing for double basses, and at the opposite extreme for the piccolos playing open fifths low down in their compass or doubling the clarinets at three and the bass clarinet at four octaves' distance. Particularly arresting, however, are the last pages with the semitonal clashes for drums, a four part double-bass *divisi*, dissonant polytonal harmonies for string and harps, and over it all an exquisitely poignant melodic line for the voice, rising and falling like the flight of a wounded bird.

Technical advances in the manufacture of instruments and in their handling were inspired by the changing character of music, but also by the general impulse to technological development consequent on the rapid growth of technical and mechanical skill which in the nineteenth century industrialized Europe. In the second phase of industrialization and mechanization in which we live the same influences are strong. Instrumental expression and an interest in virtuosity for its own sake still show musicians, and their allies the instrument-makers, unwilling to be left out of the van of technological progress.

Romanticism and urbanization, meeting with the forces of militant democracy, gave the other commanding force in nineteenth-century music: the audience. Therefore another problem arose, which may be stated in familiar terms: we must give the audience what it wants, or rather, what it expects. The composer was by now under obligation to a new patronage. Aristocratic patrons survived, it is true, but the guarantee of security for a nineteenth-century composer lay in the sale of sheet music to thousands of willing singers and players. Part-songs, anthems, piano music, arrangements for domestic musical ensembles proliferated, and all reflected—often at a much lower level—the moods and idioms of the large-scale musical forms of the concert hall. Church music, therefore, was generally divertingly secular, and music for children usually an echo of what was thought proper for adults.

England became unmusical precisely at that point in her history when music was cultivated more widely—though not more deeply—than ever before. For practical purposes England in the nineteenth century was dead: that is to say English composers meant absolutely nothing to Continental musicians. Many minor composers prospered materially, but they abdicated their responsibility to lead rather than be led by common sentiment. Economic power and relative prosperity mingled with a reluctance to revolt bred a complacency that is summed up in the adjective "Victorian", and represented in almost every musical work composed by a native composer. The turning-point came when three composers arrived on the scene. Although they were strongly influenced by the universal German romantic idiom, they were determined on independence of thought. Parry, Stanford, and particularly Elgar each in his own way determined to illuminate English thought and life with English music in an English idiom—with the qualification that Stanford was an Irishman and a devout believer in the theory that

England is all the better from an infusion of Irishry. Each was staunchly nationalist.

That brings us to a final issue, and perhaps the most significant, in mature Romantic philosophy. From the principle that the individual is important in himself, and by himself, grew the theory of national significance. This was enunciated in one way or another by a succession of German philosophers—Kant, Fichte, Hegel, and Nietzsche, all of whom had some considerable influence on the outlook of Richard Wagner. A corporate significance implied a corporate identity: thus Italy and Germany, the large and influential confederations of states variously governed but bound, in each case, by ties of language, aspired to unity. In the one case unity was symbolized by the operas of Wagner, in the other by those of Giuseppe Verdi.

Wagner, whose family was put to flight by the invasion of Saxony by the armies of Napoleon in 1813, took all German thought and music, past and present, as his province. Sure in his own destiny and convinced of his value to his compatriots (both of which made him a difficult person in any social or business relationship) Wagner made opera into "music drama", which in him was elevated almost to the status of a secular religion, with its temple in the Festival Theatre at Bayreuth. The romanticism of Wagner lies first in his looking back to ancient times, to the splendid, colourful, heroic middle ages of *Tannhäuser* and *Lohengrin*, to the pleasantries of sixteenth-century Nürnberg in *The Meistersinger*; next in his exposition of Nordic mythology in the great four-drama sequence of *The Nibelung's Ring*, which also seems in some symbolic, even prophetic, way to outline the rise and fall of human society; in his scrutiny of intimate human relationships in *Tristan and Isolde*; finally in his apparent renunciation of worldly values and acceptance of an authoritative spiritual authority in the last, religious, drama of *Parsifal*.

Wagner set out with a mission in life: to become a man of influence on German affairs. He succeeded. The measure of his Romantic success—as philosopher through music—is exemplified by his inclusion in the index of Bertrand Russell's *History of Western Philosophy*. He is, in fact, the only composer mentioned by the author in that book.

The music of Wagner was taken as a symbol of the strength and greatness of the new unified Germany, that under the guidance of Bismarck, and after Prussian military victories over Austria and France, was otherwise marked by the assumption of the title "German Emperor" by King William of Prussia in January 1871.

The Festival Theatre, Bayreuth, Royal Box

A little more than a year later, in July 1872, King Victor Emmanuel marched into Rome to take possession of the new capital (released from papal temporal rule) of an Italy that had become unified, principally through the endeavours of Garibaldi and Cavour, and the hatred of so many Italian patriots of domination by France and Austria.

As in Germany, so in Italy; there were writers and philosophers to point ideals: of these the most celebrated was Alessandro Manzoni. Manzoni exercised an influence in Italy similar to that of Goethe in Germany, and was hailed as the greatest Italian writer of modern times; first because he was a prophet of liberty (Manzoni thought the English under-valued Byron); second because his revivification of olden times (he was a disciple of Walter Scott) gave depth to the concept of unity; third because he was applauded outside Italy. Manzoni died in 1873. A year later a splendid memorial was raised to his memory by Giuseppe Verdi in the shape of a *Requiem Mass*, first performed in the Church of St. Mark in Milan.

Verdi himself was hardly less revered than Manzoni. His operas, the subjects of some such as *I Lombardi* and *Ernani* deliberately chosen to reflect the political temper of the Italian people, caught the imagination of his compatriots by their fire, their energy, and their directness of appeal. He learned much from Donizetti, Bellini, and Rossini (whose Biblical opera *Mosè* served as a model for his own *Nabucco*) and worked within an idiom that was generally understood. At the same time, although the reforms of Gluck had had virtually no effect in Italy, Verdi penetrated to the heart of his characters and gave them a musical life of their own. His recommendation to the singer who was to undertake the title role in *Macbeth* may be noted; that he should "study closely the dramatic situation and the words: the music comes off by itself. In short I would prefer you to serve the poet rather than the composer."

Verdi's operas conquered Europe, as those of earlier Italians. But unlike many of his predecessors he never ceased to develop his powers, nor did he permit musical extravagance, and the whims of singers, to destroy dramatic unity and vision. Thus *Rigoletto*, *Il Trovatore*, *La Traviata*, *Un ballo in Maschera*, *La forza del destino*, *Aïda*, *Otello*, and *Falstaff* (composed in extreme old age) are as different

La Scala, Milan

from each other as the plays of Shakespeare; now catching the style of Meyerbeer in the spectacular, of Rossini in comedy, of Wagner in recognition of Wagner's orchestral genius and the dramatic point of the principle of *leit-motiv*, but all consistent in their melodic vitality. Verdi believed that nothing could capture the attention of an audience like the human voice. In this respect, he stood as the antithesis, or the complement, to Wagner, whose approach to the problem of opera was through symphony, and, being through symphony, acknowledged the overall authority of those abstract principles that impose order on the world of music.

Society is based on a balance; on the one hand liberty, and on the other discipline. This balance is ideal rather than actual, and as a rule either one of those elements outweighs the other, with consequences that are often disastrous. The same elements, which are abstract, are also at the root of art. Sometimes the predominance of the one particular principle is directly and consciously reflected in art; sometimes not. A composer (like everyone else) is always himself a battlefield. He can choose between order or disorder, between discipline and freedom, between what are classified as classical and romantic. A composer living in a so-called classical period is pulled one way by the general climate of music, and vice versa. But the classical composer, such as Haydn, may well find the romantic traits in his own character a compulsive force: in this case he will attempt to achieve his own synthesis of ideas and ideals.

In the nineteenth century, the composer was born into a romantic atmosphere. In every case, however, it was realized that undisciplined music was impracticable. No one would play or listen to it. We have now so far developed that the same prohibitions no longer prevail.

The classical master of the late Romantic era was Johannes Brahms, whose symphonies, concertos, and chamber music were accepted as the natural appendix to those of Beethoven. In such music Brahms observed the classical principles of structure. His formal disposition of sound was intelligible within the Haydn-Mozart-Beethoven system. He was conservative in regard to colour, and the relative austerity of his orchestration was respected as virtue. If Brahms's symphonies are of sandstone, in contrast to the granite of Beethoven, they are still symphonies. Of course Brahms could not fail to express emotion; but the emotion is impersonal rather than personal, general rather than particular.

Brahms composed according to German habit. He was a song-writer, hardly less important in this sphere than Schumann; a poetical writer of keyboard music, and a choral writer of more significance than is acknowledged in a period in which choral music is relegated to an inferior position. His attitude to art was that of former times. He was primarily a craftsman who would express himself through his craft, rather than an expressionist who found a medium through which to voice his views. He possessed the "high seriousness", which Matthew Arnold—an artist who tried not dissimilarly to solve the same dilemma in which he found himself—defined as the most necessary quality of art. It is no accident that the works which, perhaps, attract the most contemporary critical scrutiny are those in which this quality is most evident: the first, third and fourth symphonies, the "Alto Rhapsody" and the *Four Serious Songs*. There are few major works by Brahms which do not show darkness as well as light.

On the technical side Brahms recognized that harmony was not a sufficient end in itself. Having explored the possibilities of symphony, and of the air and variations form (which reached an apex of achievement in the Paganini, Handel, and Haydn variations), he retired further back in time to study anew the method of Bach. The contrapuntal principles of that composer agreed with his interpretation of the relationship between discipline and freedom, and he applied them anew within the context of his own experience. This, again, is frequently evident. The finale of the fourth symphony is a magnificent *passacaglia*, and it is based on a theme derived from one of Bach's church cantatas. More particularly attention should be drawn to the great motets (Op. 29, 74, 110) and to the final sequence of chorale preludes for the organ.

Brahms expressed himself with some asperity on the "new music" of his day. He found it difficult to appreciate that of Wagner, and easy to dislike that of Liszt. Although he applauded the *Requiem* of Verdi, he had no great affection for Italian opera. He was regarded by many as hopelessly reactionary. By pursuing his ideal in respect of craftsmanship, however, he proved himself to be in fact more progressive than the progressive; looking forward to a revival of concern for the texture of music itself, and for its value as a channel for intellectual as well as emotional energy. A German—he was born in Hamburg—who lived his later life in Vienna, Brahms appears to amalgamate the sternness of the north with the grace of the Austrian capital. In this, too, he resembles Beethoven.

The other outstanding symphonic composer of the same epoch was Tchaikovsky, the composer who brought within the ambit of Western formal design the fire, the energy, the pathos, of Russia. It is not inconvenient that Tchaikovsky's "box-office" draw is the "1812" overture, first performed in Moscow seventy years after the event which it memorialized. Here is programme music *par excellence*—with the incorporation of cannon-fire, of bells (which had been used previously in Russia in the *Te Deum* composed by Giuseppe Sarti in honour of Potemkin's capture of Otchakov in the Turkish War of 1787), and of Alexis Lvov's Imperial Hymn. The immediate effect of this music is overpowering. So too with Tchaikovsky's other major works, which possess a consistent vividness beyond what any of his contemporaries could produce.

After the repulse of Napoleon and the harrowing retreat from Moscow, Russia, under the great Alexander I, enjoyed an enhanced prestige and power. The aftermath of Napoleonic aggression (as, later, of Hitlerite invasion) was an increase of national pride. Russian opera, like German opera, broke away from the Italian—which had been brought to a high level of brilliance and efficiency by Sarti and other visiting Italians. Glinka, Dargomizhsky, Cui, Balakirev, and Mussorgsky made Russian national opera, not without much opposition from a conservative aristocracy, by allying themselves with the writers of the Russian renaissance, especially Pushkin, by adapting frequent legends of Russian heroes of the past to libretti, by saturating themselves in folk-music idioms, and by exploiting the colour effects available from the orchestra. In this respect Berlioz was a considerable inspiration. The most notable works of this school are Glinka's *A Life for the Czar* (1836), Dargomizhsky's *Roussalka* (1856) and *The Stone Guest* (completed after the composer's death by Rimsky-Korsakov), and Mussorgsky's *Boris Godunov* (1874). Cui and Balakirev were conspicuous also in other fields and, influenced by Liszt, as well as Berlioz, spread Russian folk-music idiom across symphonic poems, chamber and pianoforte music, and song.

There were, on the other hand, those to whom musical nationalism was repugnant. Alexander Serov, for instance, was a keen Wagnerian and attempted to compose

Russian opera in accordance with Wagnerian principles; while Anton and Nicholas Rubinstein—the former only less famous as a pianist in the international field than Lizst —were convinced that the German academic tradition (as established at Leipzig) was the height of perfection.

Anton Rubinstein composed five piano concertos and six symphonies. As director of the Russian Musical Society in Moscow he undertook first performances of a number of Tchaikovsky's works. Tchaikovsky, he felt, was in the great European tradition a classical composer. So, in a sense, he was, as the force of his symphonic works and his chamber music, and the manner of his miniatures, testify; equally, however, Tchaikovsky felt the vitality of the music of his nationalist predecessors, and the power of the Russian literature of his generation. Accordingly he compromised, and in so doing caught the attention of the West, his works being received enthusiastically, especially in London and New York. Six symphonies, three piano concertos, a violin concerto, numerous symphonic poems, ten operas, three ballets, and a host of works of smaller stature are an eloquent tribute to the fertility of Tchaikovsky's invention, for many of them are still indispensable to the concert promoter whose principles centre on the proposition that people should "have what they want".

An analysis of this gives the popular recipe for composition as follows: melody or tune; vigour in rhythm, but without too much intellectual play with metre; virtuoso orchestration; narrative interest; and more than a touch of "common humanity". The listener, while firmly stating that this—say the "Pathetic" symphony (No. 6) of Tchaikovsky—is, in essence, Tchaikovsky, wishes to feel that he too is a part of the "common humanity" and that in some way or other music reflects his own personal emotions. In short he allows himself the luxury of inter-pretation. So, of course, does the conductor, who likes to give free rein to his emotions. The end of romantic music then is a grand free-for-all, in which the composer may easily come off worst.

What with Wagner, Verdi, Brahms, and Tchaikovsky, not to mention their predecessors and immediate asso-ciates, it might appear that little more could be stated within the Romantic idiom. That much else was written —and still is being written—is due to two factors. The first is the independence movement in music among the previously merely colonial powers of music; the second is the greater zest for music among ordinary people, who, deprived of folk-art in urban society, look for a substitute elsewhere. For some it is provided by orchestral music, whether "light" or "serious", live or recorded.

German romanticism carried well into the twentieth century in the tone poems and operas of Richard Strauss, Austrian romanticism in the symphonies of Bruckner and Mahler. In each of these composers the element of programme was strong and in order to give full expression to the moods to be portrayed the material adjuncts of music were still further extended. Mahler's eighth symphony—a "present to the Austrian na-tion", he called

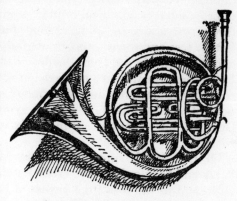

A French horn, 1870, from a photograph

it—required 8 vocal soloists, a double choir and a choir of boys, piccolo, 4 flutes, 4 oboes, cor anglais, 3 clarinets, clarinet in E flat, bass clarinet, 4 bassoons, double bassoon, 8 horns, 4 trumpets, 4 trombones, bass tuba, 3 timpani, bass drum, cymbals, gong, triangle, bells, glockenspiel, celesta, pianoforte, harmonium, organ, 2 harps, mandolin, and strings. For the performance of the work a hall had specially to be built in Munich. Truly within the general philosophic system of romantic Germany and Austria this is a work with a "message": that love is universal, as proposed by Plato and Goethe, from whose *Faust* the text of the choral part of the symphony is drawn.

In other countries there were musicians able to catch something of the primal force and fervour of Romanticism. Among them Dvořák must take a high place, for he opened new vistas of musical beauty and usually by the simplest means. Like Tchaikovsky he had a humility before the great tradition of classical music and, accepting the conventions of form endowed them with enchanting characteristics, both personal and national. In the Scandinavian countries Grieg established the right of Norway to be counted as a musical country, even though his works rarely rose above the water-colour status of brief pianoforte pieces and songs; Sibelius not only pictured Finland and its history in a splendid sequence of orchestral works, but pointed the way to a new age in the future of music by economy of utterance and of harmony, and by a revaluation of the standard design of symphonic structure; Denmark has its monument in the six symphonies of Carl Nielsen.

Of the British romantics Elgar, Mackenzie, Joseph Parry and Stanford deserve credit for their determination to present to the world the virtues of England, Scotland, Wales, and Ireland. Of these, of course, Elgar was by far the greatest, and one of no more than half a dozen British composers whose shares are quoted in the world market. Elgar was a poetical composer of supreme genius and, if personality may be said to repose in music, his impress is clearly distinguishable as individual and permanently alive. Like the great Germans, whom he so greatly admired, Elgar set out to be a master craftsman: thus he stands at least as one of the greatest of orchestrators. It is difficult to discover a better work for string orchestra than his *Introduction and Allegro,* a better or more vivid series of variations than his "Enigma", a better set of popular pieces than the *Pomp and Circumstance* marches or the "Cockaigne" overture, or a better expansion of a poem into music than is given in his setting of Cardinal Newman's *Dream of Gerontius.*

A great deal of choral music was written in the nineteenth century. Much of it was bad. A few great works stand out, among them Beethoven's *Missa Solennis,* Brahms's *Requiem,* Verdi's *Requiem,* and Elgar's *Dream of Gerontius.* That three of these were directly concerned with death is in itself a comment on the Romantic attitude.

It was, however, the *Dream of Gerontius* which gave a new lease of life to English music; for when Richard Strauss hailed it as a masterpiece the native English, who had given it a poor initial reception, thought that after this testimonial it must be. It has, therefore, joined *Messiah* and Mendelssohn's *Elijah* as a compulsory work for major choirs and music festivals.

Spain, for long a source of inspiration to composers of other nationalities, also fell back on a vast repository of folk-music, on the scenic possibilities of her ancient cities and her varied landscapes, on the literature of Cervantes, and on the musical life of the sixteenth and seventeenth centuries, and nationalist composers emerged in Pedrell (the scholar and teacher), Albéniz and Granados, and, particularly, Manuel de Falla.

Across the Atlantic music was well established in the great cities of North America, but the orchestras and opera houses of New York, Boston, Chicago, and Philadelphia were for the most part reliant on European sources, and any promising composers, like Edward MacDowell, were posted off to German academies to learn the refinements of the art of music. But when national unity, symbolized by the end of the Civil War in 1865, was established it was time to take note of qualities specifically American that might be translated into terms of music, and also to note what particular traits had developed that could be accepted as emblematic.

As early as 1781 an amateur composer, Francis Hopkinson—statesman, friend of George Washington, and one of the signatories of the Declaration of Independence—had written an opera, *The Temple of Minerva*, which was intended to popularize the idea of an alliance with France. Contemporary with Hopkinson was William Billings, of Boston. Billings was a passionate, uneducated man, consumed with religious fervour and patriotism. He composed psalm-tunes and patriotic songs, and, being indifferent to the rules by which music was supposed to be governed, was denounced by those whose only concern for music was that it should be respectable. Billings, who defended himself with relish and bad grammar, claimed the right to compose as he thought best; thus he struck a blow for complete artistic independence at an early date.

Freedom and independence of another order also inspired Stephen Foster, whose songs were a token of his regard and concern for the negro communities of the Southern states. Foster gave dignity and meaning to

The original negro minstrel, Thomas Rice as
"Jim Crow"

popular music and laid the foundations on which a later
tradition of American negro music could be built. It was
not long before negro music was investing the concert
hall and a pioneer composer in this respect was Henry
Gilbert, MacDowell's first American pupil. Gilbert's
Comedy Overture on Negro Themes and *Negro Rhapsody* are,
therefore, classics of their kind and related to Dvořák's
"New World" Symphony and "Nigger" quartet, in both
of which the Czech composer, whose visits to America

were significant experiences for him, pays his respects to a folk tradition other than his own.

American life in the nineteenth century was romantic enough from a distance: in reality it was the reverse; hard, purposeful, and practical. The spirit of the age and of the people is summed up in the poetry of Walt Whitman, both in its content and its style. Whitman, loving the "masses", who may be "turbulent, wilful", is angry with those who cling to dead things, but persuaded that good overtops bad, and that the future of America—and of the world— is in the right, energetic, hands. America, he writes,

> illustrates birth, muscular youth, the promises,
> the sure fulfilment, the absolute success, despite of
> people—illustrates evil as well as good,
> The vehement struggle so fierce for unity in one's-self;
> How many hold despairingly yet to the models departed,
> caste, myths, obedience, compulsion, and to infidelity,
> How few see the arrived models, the athletes, the western
> States, or see freedom or spirituality, or hold any faith in
> results.

Hopkinson, Billings, Foster, Sousa—the composer of popular marches—Lowell Mason the beloved hymn-writer, MacDowell, Gilbert: these were the men who began to give American music its independent character, and those who applied to it the democratic principles of the New World. Mason, for instance, addressed himself at an early stage to the adequate provision of music in the public schools of America. Combining his functions as educator and composer, he saw how music could be revitalized by once again becoming useful.

As soon as music is useful its Romantic forces are in retreat. By the end of the nineteenth century it was, in any case, clear that little more could be said within the established conventions. A new revolution was in sight.

11

A New Age

HAVING arrived thus far we may profitably pause and consider what music is, what it does, according to the record as it has been summarized in the previous chapters. We are then better able to set in perspective the problems raised by music of the twentieth century.

In the first place the art of music consists of the ordering of sounds, of arranging them into patterns such as may give satisfaction to the composer on the one hand and to the listener on the other. In this connection it should be noted that orderliness and logic expressed in whatever way give an intellectual, even an emotional, pleasure to a mind which in itself is disposed to precision and to reason. Formal perfection, whether in the organization of the buildings in a city, of the words in a sonnet, of the sounds in a sonata, of the lines in a drawing, or of the figures in a railway timetable, can in itself be termed "beautiful". In each case the organizer works with abstractions. In some he has a practical end in view, but the purposefulness of the operation has no connection with the basic conception of beauty, for beauty itself is so abstract as to be indefinable.

What is apprehended through the senses automatically affects the emotional centres of personality. High pitch, low pitch, loudness, softness, timbre, and all the variations of these properties, exercise a power that lies behind but remains apart from the main substance of the art of music.

But sounds which are ordered into particular forms must have physical existence; therefore the listener is obliged to unite both intellectual and emotional behaviour within the act of reception.

At this point it is clear that "beauty" can be in either of two aspects, or in a combination of both. The composer may be stronger on one side than the other, and so may the listener. We may find, for instance, that "classical" (that is, formalized) music is meaningless to the "romantically" disposed listener, and vice versa; or we may find an ability to appreciate the blend of both fundamentals. The great composers are found to be great because, within the idiom of their own age, they do achieve a balance as between the formal and the emotional. One side of the music of Palestrina, Purcell, Handel, Bach, Haydn, Mozart, Beethoven is "classical"; the other side is "romantic". One part, as it is said, comes from the head, the other from the heart.

The particular property of music is that it demonstrates the two poles of expression and understanding more than any other art—because it is the most abstract, the most unworldly of them all. It is the only art of which the elements are virtually useless in daily life. Music itself, however, is often taken to be useful for this very reason, and to live in *harmony* is the accepted condition of contentment. Philosophers are nervous when writing of music (because, of course, it defies any science of verbal explanation), but often pay compliments to it. When they do so they express the "magic" attributes allowed to music, and musicians, by the primitive. Since, somewhere, we are all primitive in feeling and imagination, they express a common view. Thus the Swiss writer Henri Amiel could say in his *Journal Intime* (published in 1884), "Everyone can come to a state of harmony. When he has done so he is well-ordered, and shows just as much as a flower, or the solar system, the divine thought. Harmony is self-contained and should symbolise order, law, truth; it is outside time and represents the eternal."

Some people believe that particular works of music supply the living expression of that symbol.

Music being accepted on this level may then be turned towards a practical end. The religious use music to support liturgies or to prepare the worshipper for the reception of doctrinal statements. Music makes words memorable. Music can reduce the listener to tears, or elevate him to ecstasy. A ritual fire dance would be impossible without music, for it would be rationally considered as too dangerous. Music may also be secularly useful. Since early times rulers have added to their prestige by adroit use of it, as well as of the other arts; and there is no great national or political movement of history that has not had its musical stimulus.

In a broad sense music can "communicate", it can convey ideas to the listener. Such ideas are of different nature from those conveyed by words, or pictorial images, and not to be reduced to analysis or exposition in words.

In the autumn of 1830 Mendelssohn went to Italy. In one of his letters home he wrote: ". . . we entered a plain, leaving the blue mountains behind us; the sun shone bright and warm through the foliage of the vines; the road winding through orchards, in which the trees were connected by trailing boughs . . . the carriage too seemed to *fly* over the smooth road, and towards evening we arrived at Udine, where we passed the night, where for the first time I ordered my supper in Italian, my tongue slipping as if on ice, one moment into English, and the next stumbling afresh."

That is excellent, lively verbal description. The

"Italian" symphony of 1833 is an excellent, lively symphony. It does not, however, describe Italy in the same way as do the letters which Mendelssohn wrote. At most it detaches from the scene abstract qualities such as lightness, speed, gaiety, and gives them musical symbols which we have come to accept as representing these qualities. The slow movement is said to be based on a pilgrim's hymn, but it does not describe pilgrims—what they looked like, what they talked about. It has a certain solemnity, and a sense of antiquity in the hymn-like melodic shape, that is all. But, it may be suggested, the music describes Mendelssohn. It may, or it may not. Alas! happy music does not always spring from happiness, but often the reverse. The artist is often freed from his emotions, and certainly from the stress of daily routine, by active composition. The artist often, then, is neither more nor less than a workman engaged in a craft for which he has a facility, filling the blank walls of aural existence with patterns of sound.

The romantic attitude sees the artist otherwise. In his poem *A Fairy Concert* Leigh Hunt, who was a great lover of music, recalled Gluck as one "who saw gods" when composing. Gluck would have been greatly surprised. The romantic attitude swelled up disproportionately during the Romantic era, and left musicians, if not their audiences, aware of the fact that Romantic principles carried to their logical end result in make-believe and artificiality. The extreme end of classical attitudes is also negative, for music which is all science, which is physically frail, is not music. At the same time the classical principles of form, order, economy, logic, are the more indispensable, for undisciplined romantic freedom gives eventual anarchy.

The young composer of the 1890's could go forward, or he could go backward. He could not stand still if he wished to be a composer of significance. Some composers did stand still, of course. But treading the safe conventional ways, out of date as soon as they are crystallized into "theory", is personally unsatisfying if sometimes materially profitable. This partly explains why music acceptable in its own day to predominantly conservative-minded listeners fails to last.

The progressive composers of the 1890's were in France, Claude Debussy and Eric Satie. Hitherto the history of music had appeared largely to be conditioned by Italians and Germans. French composers (César Franck, the most Romantic, being a Belgian by birth) had consistently remained a little apart from the main lines, maintaining a coolness, delicacy, and logic that run through the French tradition from at least as early as the reign of Louis XIV. Satie lived romantically and his biography makes strange reading, but he thought logically, indeed cynically. He hated pretentiousness in music, and in a succession of whimsical pieces, many for pianoforte, he showed his contempt for the pretentious in their titles and unexpected musical content. Satie struck a blow for the eccentric, but taught a salutary lesson, learned by the next generation of French composers headed by Ravel; that musical composition is fundamentally concerned with the arrangement of sounds, and that each composer may evolve his own methods of arrangement.

Debussy was a more extensive genius, owing much of his instruction to a school of painters who were also in opposition to overripe Romantic method. Among these painters were Pissarro, Manet, Degas, Renoir, and Monet, and their paintings will still be found astonishingly vivid, colourful, and—above all—light. In many cases their subjects included water, in which colours are reflected in an ever-moving but delicate kaleidoscope. These French

o   209

Impressionism: sunshine and reflections at Munich, from a picture by Reginald Haggar

painters tried to capture the movement of colour in land-
or seascape, to set down their immediate impressions.
Thus, at first slightingly, they were termed Impressionists.
They led the way to a more vital texture in painting
because they relied on the pure, bright colours of the
spectrum. Debussy tried to achieve in music what the
Impressionist painters had achieved. Lightness, delicacy,
space, the peculiar shimmering effects apparent on can-
vas were by him translated into terms of music. He
removed music from one phase of Romanticism to another.
He retained the idea of descriptiveness, but, as is clear in
his pianoforte pieces and orchestral works, his representa-

tions were pictorial rather than literary, and his aim was to capture the brightness and radiance of nature in music that was also bright, and radiant, and non-dramatic. Affinity with the Impressionist painters is suggested by many of his titles: *Gardens in the Rain*, *Reflections in the Water*, *The Submerged Cathedral*, *The Sea*, and *Clouds*.

Debussy was also acquainted with the new school of French poets known as the Symbolists, among whom were Verlaine, Baudelaire, and Mallarmé, who suggested rather than stated ideas. The union of literary Symbolism and musical Impressionism was brought about by Debussy in one of his most delicate orchestral pieces, the *Prélude*, its title taken from a poem by Mallarmé, *L'Après-midi d'un Faun*. In contrast with other music of that period this work, with unfamiliar scales and fluid rhythms, seems to "be going nowhere". It was because of this that, in another sense, it was going somewhere.

Debussy's technique may well be studied at the piano, but he was a consummate master of its sonorities. Here we may see how he lightened his chordal texture, and introduced new and strange effects by recourse to medieval modal principles, to the overtones produced by bells and other instruments, and to the "whole-tone" scale. The "whole-tone" scale was the result of Debussy's attendance at the World Fair in Paris in 1889, where he heard a Javanese group of instrumentalists play music composed within a similar scale. In such ways Debussy looked for musical colours somewhat akin to the painters' pure colours of the spectrum. He also sought to free music from the tyranny of the set metrical patterns that dominated German music, and his works are marked therefore by a new rhythmic plasticity.

Going forward often means going backward, to first principles, to the inspiration of clear thought and style.

Maurice Ravel, grouped with Debussy as an Impressionist, appreciated the singular beauty of the claveçin composers of the seventeenth century—especially Couperin, and in his music is found a re-creation of their lucid values. A characteristic example is the set of pieces entitled *Le Tombeau de Couperin*. At the same time Ravel, of Basque descent on his mother's side, was excited by the rhythms of Spanish music, which are frequent in his music. He was also an orchestrator of great skill, with no less appreciation of colour than Debussy but with something more of draughtsmanship.

The large "symphony orchestra"—so exquisitely exhibited in Ravel's ballet suites *Daphnis and Chloe*—is so much taken for granted that its importance to the modern composer is often overlooked. The great orchestras of the nineteenth century grew from those of the opera houses, but progressive municipalities established bodies of players independent of this connection. Especially was this the case in America, where orchestras are generously subsidized (a perennial problem in England) from municipal revenues and private benefactions. Of recent years the latter have frequently come from industrial sources. There have also developed other orchestras established by broadcasting authorities. Thus the individual skill of players has improved enormously and virtuoso standards are the rule rather than the exception. One of the most encouraging consequences of this has been the extension of technical proficiency to amateur orchestras (which offer fresh opportunities to the enterprising composer) and particularly to "youth" orchestras, in which the National Youth Orchestra of Great Britain has played a distinguished and pioneer role.

The modern composer, therefore, can hardly go wrong in this field, for whatever he writes will in all probability be made to sound right by more than competent playing. Sometimes the listener is tempted to listen to the playing rather than to the music. This, however, is only a new aspect of an old situation, also found in drama, where the talents of the virtuoso performer stimulate an art within an art.

In the music of the Romantic era the orchestra was treated rather more as a mass than today, because of the supremacy of harmony. In contemporary music, which is less harmonic, each player is made to feel that he has an individual part to play. This is due to a regard for all conceivable tone qualities and effects on the one hand, and to a freer conception of what constitutes an orchestra than formerly. The contemporary composer may use a complete orchestra or he may not. In this connection the scores of Igor Stravinsky make a rewarding study.

Stravinsky, indeed, is one of the great composers of modern times. Born near St. Petersburg (Leningrad) in 1882, Stravinsky followed in the tradition of Rimsky-Korsakov and earlier Russian nationalists. His reputation was established in the first place by the ballets—*The Firebird* and *Petrushka*—commissioned by Diaghilev and performed by the Russian Ballet in Paris. In 1913 Stravinsky's *Rite of Spring* was given its première. It was greeted with unrestrained hostility, for clearly Stravinsky had turned his back on the favoured romantic-nationalist tradition (much modified and clarified, however, by Stravinsky) and introduced what at that time could only be regarded as "barbarism": elemental sounds of strange provenance, unexpected but captivating rhythms beaten out with percussive intensity. Still descriptive music, but with a fearsome truth-to-nature, bearing in mind that nature is not as kind as more lyrical spirits would have us believe.

In Paris Stravinsky was closely in touch with some of the

most influential painters of the century—the Fauvists and Cubists, including Derain, Braque, Picasso and Gris, who were themselves interested in music and contributors to the designs for Diaghilev's ballets. Here it should be noted that the rise in popularity of ballet as an art form was in large measure due to Diaghilev's genius for bringing together artists, composers, and dancers of outstanding talent and originality.

In the middle period of his career Stravinsky (who exemplifies the principle that each work by a great composer is a new experience created by a mind that is continually exploring) sought to impose a greater discipline on music by recourse to the lucid and impersonal idiom of the eighteenth century. Thus he composed a series of concerto-type works and two symphonies which are distinguished more by clarity of melodic line and by a more abstract logic in structure than by "colour". However, it is clear from those and other works that Stravinsky considers that the character of the music and its purpose naturally dictate the appropriate range of colour. The delightful play with music *The Soldier's Tale* (composed during the First World War in Switzerland when meagre resources were available) requires only a handful of instruments, but this chamber ensemble of violin, double bass, clarinet, bassoon, cornet, trombone, and percussion is proportionate to the scale of the play as a whole, and therefore no lack of colour is felt; particularly since Stravinsky knows exactly of what each instrument is capable, and since his vital rhythms give a new dimension of their own. On the other hand the *Symphony of Psalms*, a three-movement choral symphony composed for the fifteenth anniversary of the Boston Symphony Orchestra, needs a large orchestra, but without the upper strings. This omission—relating to a tradition of sacred music accompanied by wind instruments that was peculiar to central Europe—lends a particular clarity of outline, and an effective, indeed compelling, union of voices and instruments.

In his latest phase Stravinsky, living in America, which became the adopted country of many great musicians during the second quarter of the twentieth century, has shown himself aware of the influence of another notable reformer—Arnold Schoenberg.

Schoenberg was a Viennese composer, largely self-taught, whose influence on modern music is out of all proportion to the amount of music he wrote, and still more to the attention given to his music by the music-loving public. He is an *eminence grise* of music. In an age in which old values are being displaced and new ones established this situation is not uncommon.

Schoenberg (like Stravinsky) was brought up in the Romantic tradition, and that of the Vienna of Bruckner and Mahler was fairly oppressive. In such early works as *Gurre-Lieder*, for solo voices, chorus, and vast orchestra, and *Verklärte Nacht*, Schoenberg expressed romantic impulses in a vocabulary extended from Wagnerian chromaticism. But he soon realized that this way was a cul-de-sac. He turned to the small forces of chamber music—hence a *Kammersymphonie*, string quartets, pianoforte music, and so on—and, at the same time, made a final break with conventional tonality. Music without a keynote, without chordal progressions based on precedent, is designated atonal. But even atonalism could be used as means of romantic extension. Thus we have the *Pierrot Lunaire* cycle of songs for female voice and instruments, in which an entirely new method of vocal presentation (midway between speech and song and therefore allied to recitative) is employed to express the psychological atmosphere of

Albert Giraud's poems. There are parellels here with the literary methods and aims of James Joyce. But Schoenberg looked not only for expressiveness, but also musical colour. Therefore, like other contemporary composers, he brought back forms particular to earlier periods such as passacaglia and canon.

Acceptance of atonality (strongly pointed at, independently, by Debussy, Satie, and Stravinsky) was one important step towards the complete freeing of composers from the clutches of nineteenth-century theory. The next step was the institution of a discipline to take its place. This evolved in the system worked out and demonstrated by Schoenberg in a number of small-scale works written in the early 1920's. In these, distinguished also by the unconventionality of the forces employed, the "twelve-note row" was introduced. Let it now be said that there are few musicians of the last decade or so whose works do not show traces of Schoenberg's influence; some more than others.

In essence the "twelve-note row" is simple to understand. There are twelve distinct sounds within each octave as played on the pianoforte, each a semitone distant from the next. Out of those sounds (taking into account that they may be transposed up or down) all music is created. The composer's problem is to give them some sort of order, but also variety. Previously, in modal or tonal music, one sound predominated, being a "key-note", to which all others were subordinate in different degrees of subjection. Classical and romantic music was based on key relationships and the composer planned his music with this in mind. As has been said, by the end of the nineteenth century it was commonly felt that everything that could be done within this system, for the time being, had been done. Therefore Schoenberg declared that the composer could construct his music on arrangements of the twelve notes without reference to tonality. The twelve sounds could be arranged in 479,081,600 different ways, so there was little chance of noticeable monotony.

Composition, according to this principle, starts with the setting down of a theme—a tone-row, in which all twelve sounds appear in an order determined by the composer. The theme will be arranged rhythmically—again as determined by the composer. Now the tone-row is available for other treatment. It may be inverted, that is, turned upside down. It may be set back to front, and that version may be inverted. The theme may be treated in canon (in any number of parts). The rhythmic pattern may be augmented (the note values lengthened), or diminished (shortened). So far all is linear, horizontal. But the notes may be grouped perpendicularly, thus giving rise to new chords which are directly derived from the tone-row. Is the result music? The answer to that depends on what the listener expects of music. Here it can only be said that composers of genius have created exciting musical experiences based on their exploration of the possibilities of the Schoenbergian principle. Of these composers the most outstanding is Alban Berg, an Austrian disciple of Schoenberg, whose Violin Concerto and opera *Wozzeck* are accepted as classics of the new order.

A personal note may be intruded. Young students of composition have derived great satisfaction from studying the "twelve-note row", and by considering the capabilities of any medium they choose to employ have composed works of far more compelling quality than by adhering strictly to the older methods of composition technique which are still, too stringently, insisted on by those whose primary consideration is that young composers should write what their elders think they "like". The technique of composition comes from self-discipline, but also from a zest for tonal exploration. Likewise the art of listening comes from similar roots: the listener must train himself to appreciate that a composer is one who has something to present other than what the listener would express if he could!

At the same time there must be a union between composer and listener, and between both and the performer. This brings us to another cardinal issue in contemporary music, and indeed contemporary art as a whole. According to modern political philosophers the "ordinary man" has an important contribution to make to the community as a whole. While this is a consequence of Renaissance and then of Romantic philosophy, and social theory, the putting into practice of the theory on a large scale (as by universal suffrage) is a feature of twentieth-century organization. The putting into practice is both exciting and, at times, disillusioning; but, since we are at the beginning rather than the end of a chapter, misadventures are to be expected.

The arts depend on patrons. In former times musicians depended on churches, courts, and private individuals for their sustenance. Now that is no longer the case. The composer depends on the public. To be more precise, he depends on the organs and organizations which represent the public; either directly, as in the case of department of state or local government, or indirectly, as in the case of semi-autonomous but subsidized bodies such as opera houses, symphony orchestras, the film industry, or broadcasting corporations.

The record of patronage of arts through the ages is one largely of compromise. The patron has his likes and dislikes as well as his pocket to consider. In general, then, he has defined the purpose for which he requires music, or

Television: the orchestra in the home

painting, or poetry; less often he has indicated the style
which the artist should adopt. On the other hand the
artist, jealous of the independence of his craft and his
ideas, wishes to work out his own artistic destiny. To do
what he wants to do and yet to oblige his patron—on
whose willingness to pay the artist depends for his livelihood—calls from the artist a sense of accommodation. But
there is more to it than that: by such consideration art is
rendered intelligible, and set within the framework of
common life.

The twentieth century is often described—hopefully—
as the "age of the common man". The aim of education-
ists in every country in the Western world, at least, is to
make music available for everyone: hence it is encouraged

in schools. Too often, perhaps, music that is studied and practised belongs to yesterday rather than to today: there is a general tendency to prefer creative musicians dead rather than alive.

In the days of Bach, a composer wrote for whatever forms, vocal or instrumental, were to hand. At the present time two out of every three composers declare that they have been influenced by Bach. Music, since the dethronement of harmony, has become more contrapuntal, less inclined to expose instrumental colour for the sake of colour, more abstract, more "scientific" and less assuredly "inspired". Schoenberg quotes Bach as the great exemplar, and so did Vaughan Williams, and so do many other composers. The *concerto grosso* type of work is again in vogue. The American composers Virgil Thomson and Roy Harris looked back to the eighteenth century and produced a *Symphony on a Hymn Tune* (a kind of extended American chorale prelude) and a fine *Passacaglia-Cadenza-Fugue* respectively; in Béla Bartók's *Music for Strings, Percussion and Celesta* the first movement is a fine and exciting fugue; the Swiss composer Frank Martin shows eighteenth-century affinities in his *concertante* works, in which only a small number of instruments are employed, and in the oratorio *Golgotha*, commissioned by the Genevan Broadcasting Company to mark the end of the Second World War.

In the mid-nineteenth century pictorial artists looked behind Romanticism and found new values in Renaissance painting. The contemporary composer often also looks behind the Romantic era and his style may well show influences stretching back from Bach to the Middle Ages. But there is another point besides that of style. Before the Romantics climbed on the shoulders of Rousseau towards the rare atmosphere of "art for art's sake", composers thought in terms of utility. Once again the contemporary composer seeks creative opportunity in utility, and is sometimes prepared to consider no musical task, however slight, discreditable. "Functional" architecture is possible: "functional" music not quite so possible, but composers do their best to give the impression that it might be.

Benjamin Britten writes works for schoolchildren, Leonard Bernstein for Broadway "musicals". The pioneer

Modern metal sculpture outside the Stedelijk Museum, Amsterdam

in modern "utility" music, however, was Paul Hindemith, who, influenced by the German Bach tradition,
expressed his views, which were supported by many
works designed for social occasions, in the 1920's. Hindemith considered that a composer should be a citizen, in
the fullest sense of the word, as well as a composer, and
that his works should reflect his concern for the affairs in
which he is involved. Hindemith, who was compelled like
many other European musicians in the 1930's to leave his
own country and make a new life in America, is a prolific
composer and writer, and a teacher. His music ranges from
the opera *Matthis der Maler* (parts of which have been
formed into a symphony of the same name), by way of
much orchestral music composed for differing combina-
tions and chamber music, to keyboard music, songs, and
musical plays and cantatas for amateur and school ensembles. The style of Hindemith's music is direct and
plain-spoken, and analogous to that of much contemporary prose and verse which avoids flowery phrases and
pretentious utterance.

Utility and directness of expression are encouraged
among those communities which are most prominent in
promoting the idea of music for all. Thus both in America
and the countries in the Soviet zone of interest high schools,
sporting organizations, and cultural groups sponsored by
Trade Unions attract the attention of leading composers,
such as Aaron Copland on the one hand and Dmitri
Shostakovitch on the other. In Britain there are opportunities still waiting. Competitive musical festivals particularly should give rise to new and vital music, but their
organizers will need to escape the prejudice that modern
music is reserved for special people in special places, and
composers to realize that herein is a challenge. The dismal
part is, of course, that English music is, and for most of its

existence has been, dominated by what goes on in London. In no other country is national taste so subordinate to that of the capital city.

New ideas and new styles do not, as a rule, exist by themselves and without relation to those of former times. The Romantic need is no longer subscribed to in the same manner as in the Romantic era, but its influence is still considerable and the romantic traits of art are irrepressible, even, paradoxically, in anti-Romanticism.

Much contemporary music is strongly national in character—which is often as good a way of ensuring its international significance as any other. At the head of the national list stand many works by twentieth-century Russian composers. Among the compositions of Shosta-kovitch (one of the leading symphonists of the present day) are operas, ballets, choral works, and large-scale works for orchestra which are intended to celebrate the achievements of the U.S.S.R. Aram Khatchaturian links more directly the present with the past in making considerable use of folk-music idiom. In the U.S.A. such composers as Aaron Copland, Roy Harris, and Randall Thompson are no less concerned to present a distinctively national impression. In both cases—even though composers have differing styles and techniques—the intention is roughly the same: to create music for the "common man".

The music of Béla Bartók—one of the outstanding composers of modern times—is, although highly individual, never far from romantic impulses, in that his zest for transferring Hungarian folk-idiom into terms of art music and his sense of musical colouring are always apparent.

There are, of course, many occasions when the composer must draw from his romantic sensibility. Opera is the most romantic of musical forms of expression—because fundamentally it represents a union of the romantic

The temptation of St. Anthony, adapted from Jerome Bosch

elements (this is the meeting-point) in all the contributing arts. Thus such varied operas as Ravel's *L'heure espagnole*, Berg's *Wozzeck*, Kurt Weill's *Die Dreigroschenoper* (The Threepenny Opera), Vaughan Williams's *Riders to the Sea*, Britten's *Peter Grimes*, Gian-Carlo Menotti's *The Consul*, Wolfgang Fortner's *Bluthochzeit*, and Hindemith's *Harmonie der Welt* are all powerful in emotional impact.

The ways in which composers achieve their ends, however, are very various; and this is where the listener is sometimes at sea. It is often remarked that music is a universal language. So it is, in the sense that its understanding and enjoyment (the two are inseparable) do not depend on localized verbal phrases, and that organized musical sounds will stimulate some response, whether of pleasure or pain, without the listener being compelled to reply to the message in the same currency. Moreover from the late Middle Ages until the end of the nineteenth century musical technique in western Europe was homogeneous. For the most part composers used the same medium—concerto grosso, symphony, symphonic poem, opera, oratorio, chamber music—in the same general way. Also composers, whatever their race, shared the same general view as to the purpose of music.

This, however, is an age of specialization. One composer will settle exclusively for this system or that. There are "twelve-note row" composers, there are tonal composers, there are composers who do without harmony, others (following Anton Webern) who do without melody. Some write "popular" music, others write only "serious" music; still others try to combine both. *Musique concrète* is one form of modern music—not wholly dissimilar to "action painting". Here the principle is to tape-record noises (as of machinery or anything else that is available), to edit the recording, and then to present it as a musical work. Electronic music (much cultivated in Germany and Italy) is another form of modern music, in which composers twiddle knobs that control electronic valves and produce strange results that usually defy either explanation or analysis except in mathematical terms. But, so long as the experimentalists do not take themselves too seriously (which they are inclined to do), no great harm is done: after all the aim of the musician is to harness sound, to master it, and to turn the raw material into a finished product. There are no limits to the raw materials of the art; so a composer may legitimately explore all the possibilities.

The scientific properties of the technological age are thus apparent at every turn. There is a scientific attitude towards sound, there is a scientific attitude towards composition; which is only another way of saying that classicism is a lively force.

That takes us back to where we started—or nearly. As soon as music becomes organized it shows intellectual and emotional aspects. These are always present.

So we may view music from the outside. But music is not only to be admired from a distance, for as well as being an art it is a social act. We listen to music, but we also make it. Until comparatively recently an audience was composed of people whose responses were guided by their own practical experience. Thus there was a close link between the artist and his public, and the latter could better understand what the former was setting out to achieve. If the gap between artist and patron widens further the next stage of art is not encouraging. The artist will merely be another among a growing body of specialists telling us what to do and what to like. Modern music, no more than any other, needs no special pleading or copious explanation. It needs the active participation of those for whom it is, or should be, made.

The patron of arts wields great responsibility, for he keeps them, and the artists, alive. The present patron of the arts is—you.

APPENDIX

Works to Study

THE following list of recorded music relates only to the first six and last chapters. To compile a comprehensive table containing all the composers dealt with in the book would be impracticable. At the same time the reader may easily discover records of music from the eighteenth and nineteenth centuries (recordings of present-day music are discussed in the newspapers—in some better than others) for himself: to this end he is advised to read either the monthly issue of *The Gramophone*, the quarterly issue of *The Gramophone—Long Playing Classical Record Catalogue*, or both. (Set the index of the latter against the General Index of this book and see what you can find.)

"Old music" and "folk-music" are sometimes available in arrangements, or they sometimes form the basis of a new work—as in the case of Britten's *The Young Person's Guide to the Orchestra*. Music of this kind may often stimulate an interest in the unfamiliar and also demonstrate that "new" and "old" are relatively unimportant terms in musical appreciation. Despite what is sometimes said, arrangements are only bad if they are indifferent (*i.e.* unmusical) arrangements; not because they are arrangements. Therefore a few arrangements are included below.

I

Examples of ancient instrumental and vocal music from the Far and Middle East are available in Volume I of the *History of Music in Sound*: HMV, HLP 1.

Detailed information about such music, as well as musical excerpts, may be found in the *Historical Anthology of Music*, A. T. Davison and W. Apel (pub. Harvard University Press and OUP).

An excellent collection of rare and exotic instruments is maintained in the Horniman Museum, South London, by the London County Council, from whom a catalogue (*Musical Instruments*) is obtainable.

African music from Tanganyika, Kenya, Uganda, and the Congo: Decca, LF 1084, 1120–1, 1169–73.

Folk-songs from Vietnam: Supraphon, suep 592.

Indian folk-music: HMV, ALP C2, C7, 1165; also Argo, RG 62 and Columbia 33SX1115.

II

Jewish liturgical music: HMV, HLP 1.

Ambrosian chant: Vox, DL 343.

Gregorian chant: Archive, AP 13005, APM 14002, 14017, 14034, 14104–5; also Decca, LXT 2704–8, LXT 5171, LXT 5251, and LXT 5226–7.

Liturgical drama with music, *Quem quaeritis?*: HMV, HLP 3.

III

Music of the Middle Ages, and the early Renaissance period, is extensively recorded by the Pro Musica Antiqua ensemble of Brussels:

Archive, HPM 14018–9, 14032, 14042, 14063, 14068–14069, and Archive, epa 37002–3, and epa 37057.

Angelus ad virginem: Vanguard, PUL 7046.

Mariam matrem (Spanish hymn of fourteenth century): HMV, ALP 1393.

A modern work based on medieval poems—*Carmina Burana*, Carl Orff: Columbia, 33CX1480.

IV

Ballads and madrigals of Francesco Landino: Archive, APM 14019.

Secular and sacred music of Guillaume de Machaut: Archive, APM 14063.

Motets by Guillermus Dufay: Archive, APM 14019.

Motets by John Dunstable: Archive, APM 14069.

Glogauer Liederbuch (1460)—songs with accompaniments by recorders, viols, lutes, etc.: Archive, APM 14512.

V

Hymns of this period are published in the standard hymnals, a particularly wide selection appearing in *Songs of Syon* (pub. Schott): instrumental music is increasingly available, especially in collections under the imprint of Bärenreiter, Breitkopf, Mercury, Peters, Schirmer, Schott, and Stainer and Bell.

Byrd: *Fantasie*, for viols: Vanguard, PUL 7035.

       Goe from my Window, for lute: Vanguard PUL 7032.

Cabézon: *Tiento I, III*, for harpsichord: HMV, ALP 1518.

Giovanni Gabrieli: *In ecclesiis*, for voices and instruments: HMV, HLP 9.

Le Jeune: Songs: Brunswick, AXTL 1048.

Marenzio: Madrigals: Archive, APM 14045.

Palestrina: *Stabat Mater*: Vox, PL 9740.

Prætorius: Chorales for brass: Cantate, t7167 1f.

English music of the period is well represented in all its forms in Oiseau-Lyre, OL 50130-1; Vanguard, PUL 7027, 7032, 7035; Archive, APM 14056; and Columbia, 33SX 1078.

Britten: *Variations on Sellenger's Round*: Decca, LXT 2798.

Mendelssohn: *Reformation Symphony* (last movement based on Luther's "Reformation" chorale): Mercury, MMA 11032.

Vaughan Williams: *Fantasia on a theme of Thomas Tallis*: Capitol, P 8383.

VI

Caccini: Songs: Decca, LW 5245.

Corelli: *12 Sonatas* (Op. 5): Archive, APM 14024.

          Concerto grosso (No. 8), with a concerto by Vivaldi: Archive, AP 13046.

Couperin: *Suites* (*Ordres*) 138, 191, 192: Archive, ALP 1518.

Dowland: Songs: Vanguard, PVL 7027.

Frescobaldi: Toccatas I–IX: Vox, PL 8780; Vanguard, PVL 7052.

Froberger: *Canzona, Capriccio, Fantasia, Ricercari,* and *Toccate*: Vox, DL 223.

Lully: Ballet—*Le Temps de la Paix*: Oiseau-Lyre, OL 50136.

Monteverdi: Opera—*Orfeo*: Archive, APM 14057–8.

Purcell: Anthem—*O grant the King a long life*: Decca, LXT 2798.

          Fantasias for viols: Archive, APM 14027.

          Ode for St. Cecilia's Day—*Hail, bright Cecilia*: Nixa, NCL 16021.

          Opera—*The Fairy Queen*: Oiseau-Lyre, OL 50139–41.

Schütz: *Christmas Story* (or *Oratorio*): Oiseau-Lyre, OL 50020.

          Motets: Archive, APM 14131.

Britten: *Variations on a Theme of Henry Purcell* (*Young Person's Guide to the Orchestra*): HMV, BLP 1101.

XI

This selection is of the less obvious music which might not be on view in the local dealer's, but which shows some aspects of modern music not to be overlooked.

Berg: *Violin Concerto*: Columbia, 33C1030.

Copland: Ballet—*Rodeo* (with Bernstein: Ballet—*Fancy Free*): Capitol P 8196.

Hindemith: *Mathis der Maler* (symphony based on opera): HMV, ALP 1597.

Martin: *Petite symphonie concertante*: Decca, LXT 2631.

Satie: *3 Gymnopédies*, arr. for Orchestra: Philips, SBR 6234.

Schoenberg: *Kammersymphonie*: Vox, PL 10460.

Pierrot lunaire: Argo, RG 54.

Theme and variations for wind band: Mercury, MMA 11026.

Shostakovich: Concerto for piano, trumpet, and orchestra: Parlophone, PMC 1023.

Stravinsky: *Histoire du soldat*: HMV, ALP 1377.

The Rake's Progress, Philips, ABL 3055–7.

Virgil Thomson: *Louisiana Story*: Brunswick, AXTL 1022.

Weill: Excerpts from *Der Dreigroschenoper*: Brunswick, LAT 8020.

Electronic music by Eimert, Stockhausen, and Křenek: Deutsche Grammophon, LP 16132–4.

General Index